I0461866

Real World Colouring Book

For Advanced Users & Adults

50 Images

Created From Real Life Photos For You To Colour As You Please.

ISBN 978-0-359-86315-0
90000
9 780359 863150

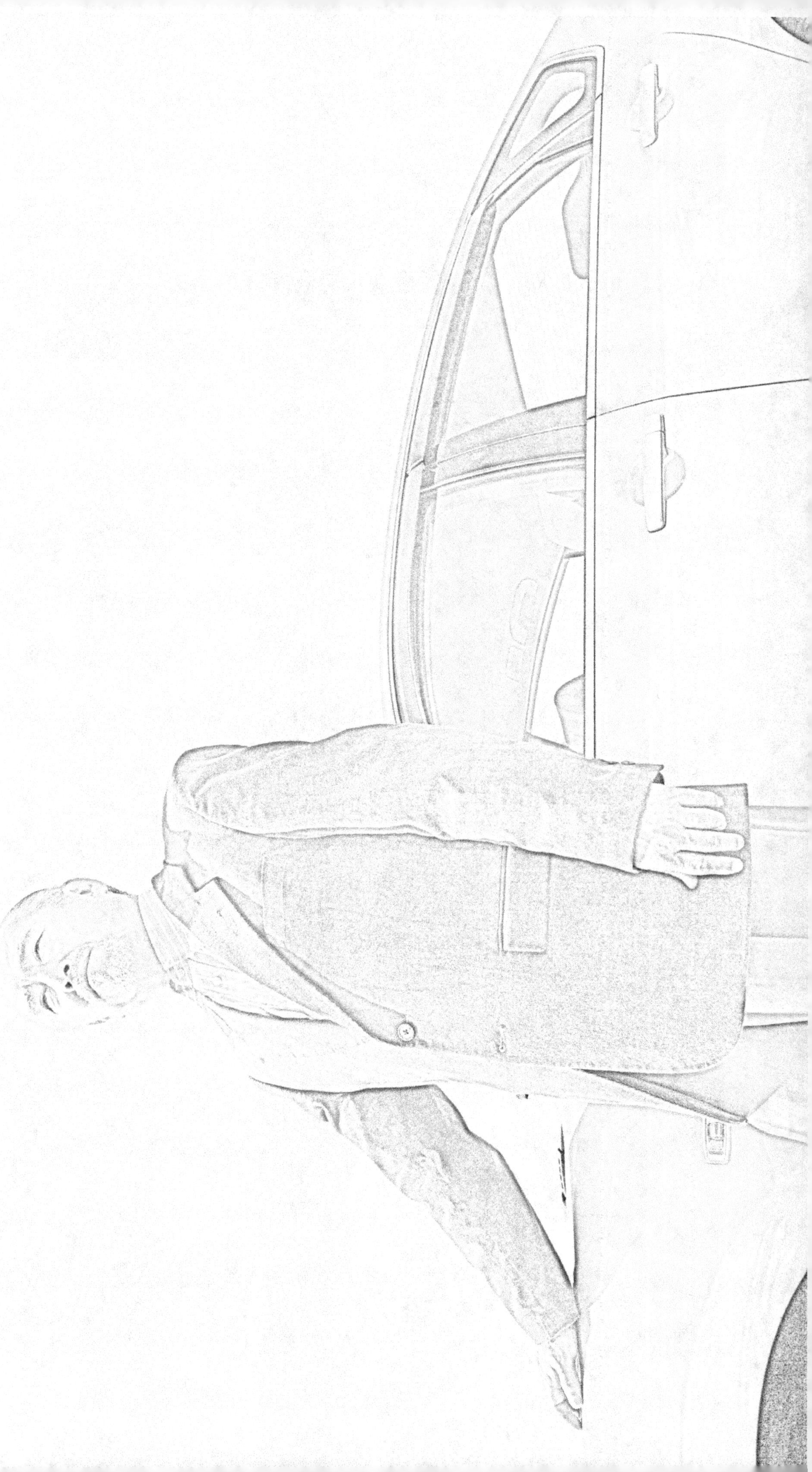

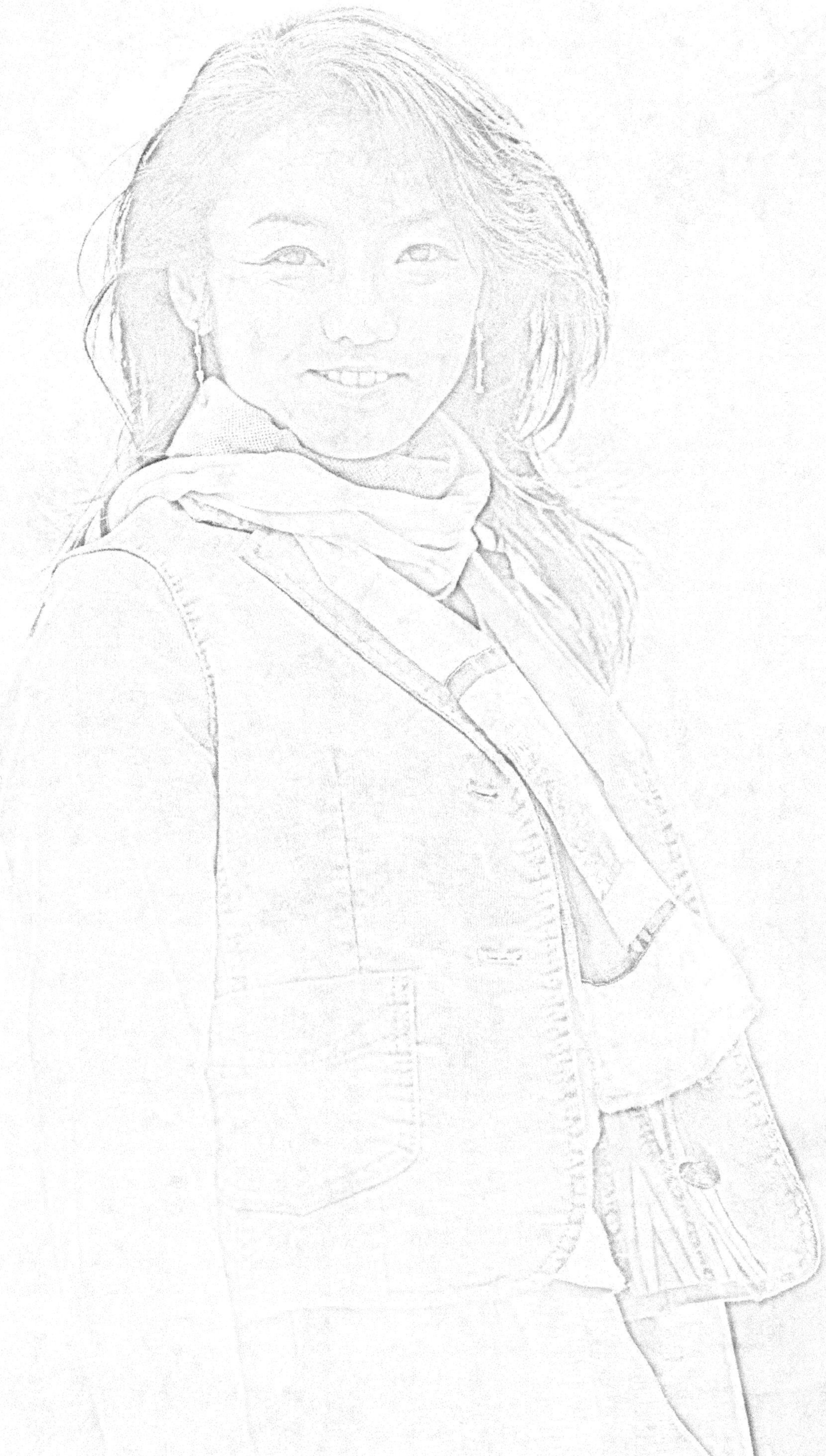

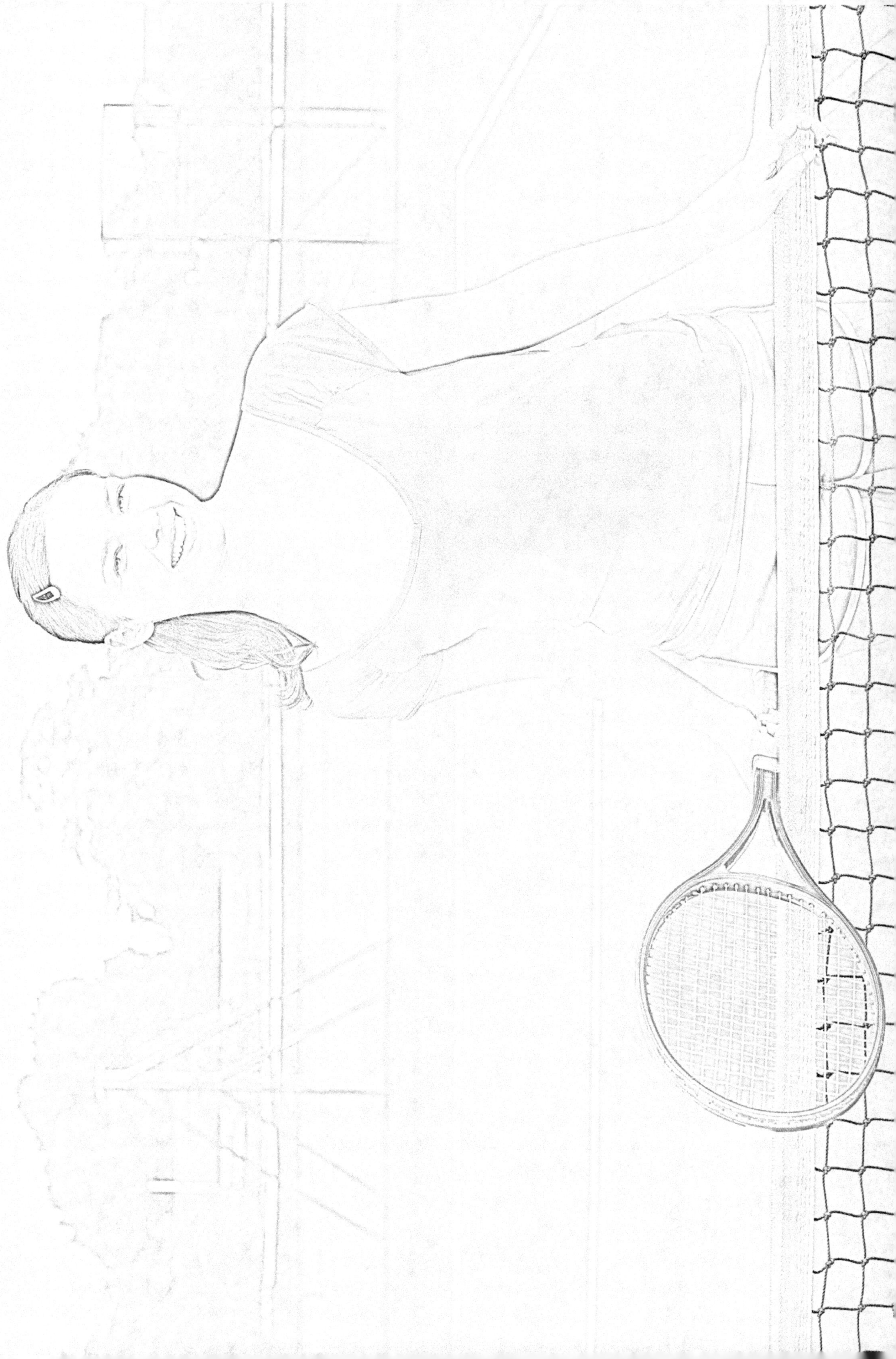

POST

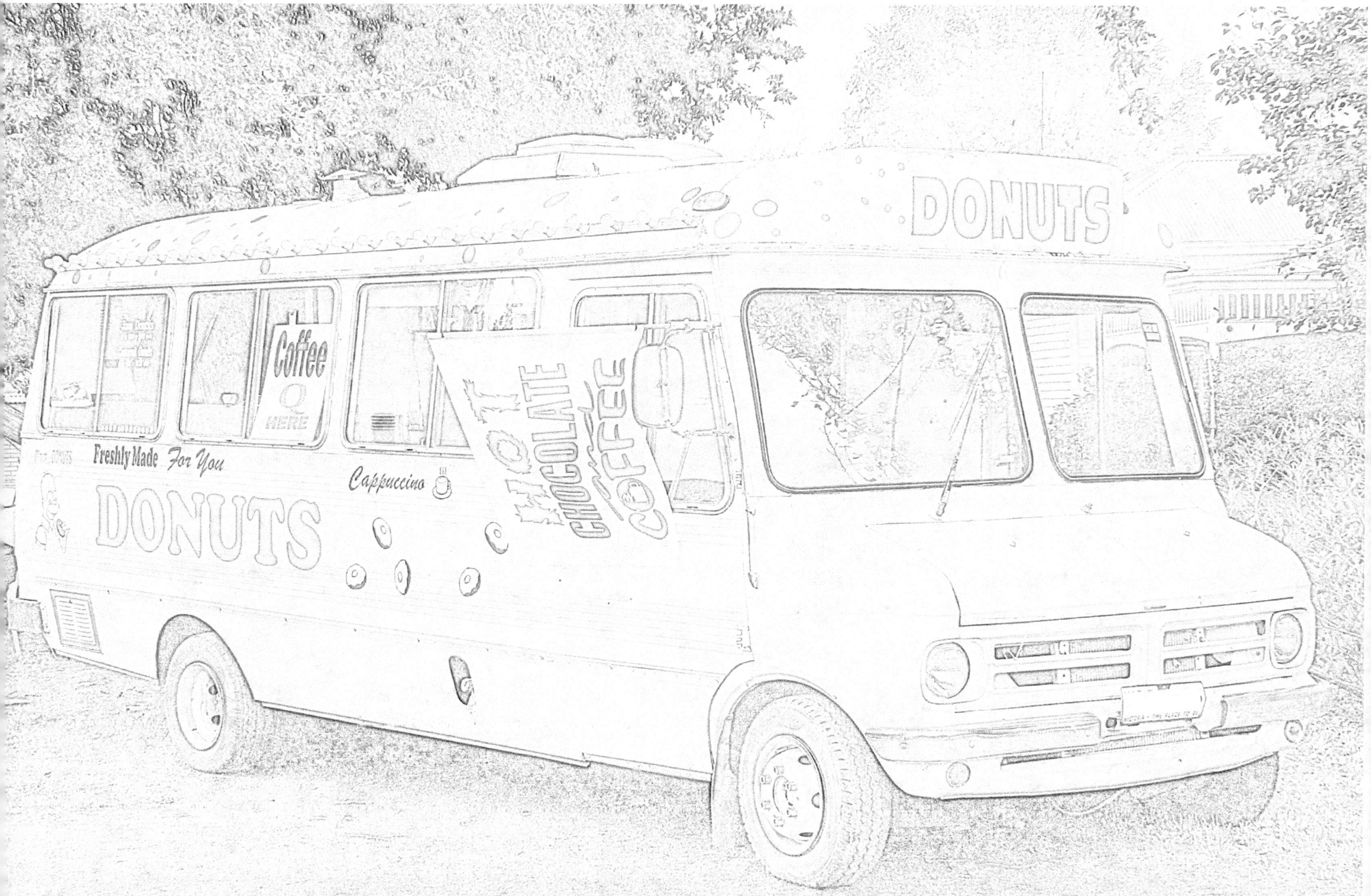
DONUTS
Coffee
Q
HERE
Freshly Made For You
DONUTS
Cappuccino
HOT
CHOCOLATE
and
COFFEE

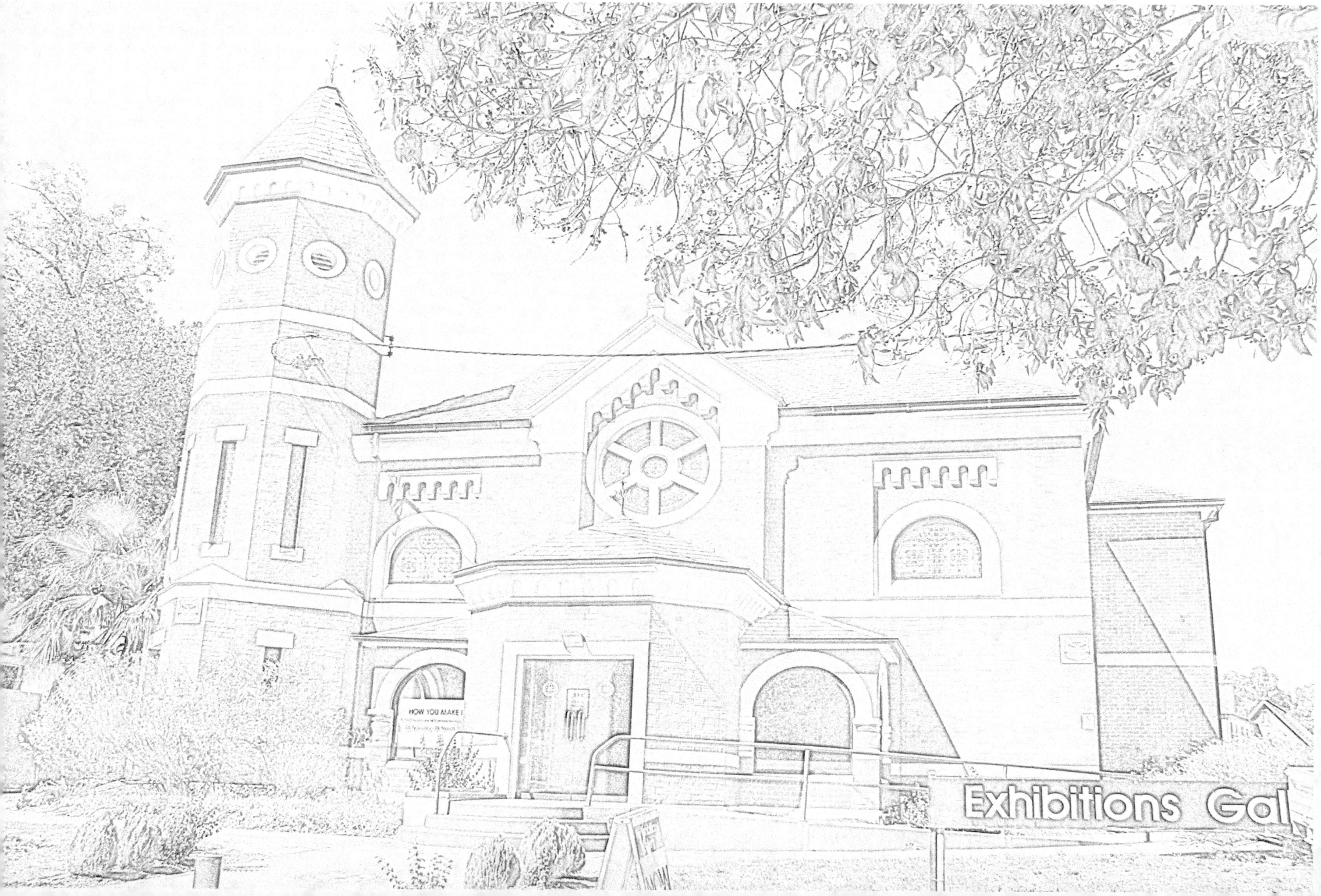
HOW YOU MAKE I
Exhibitions Gal

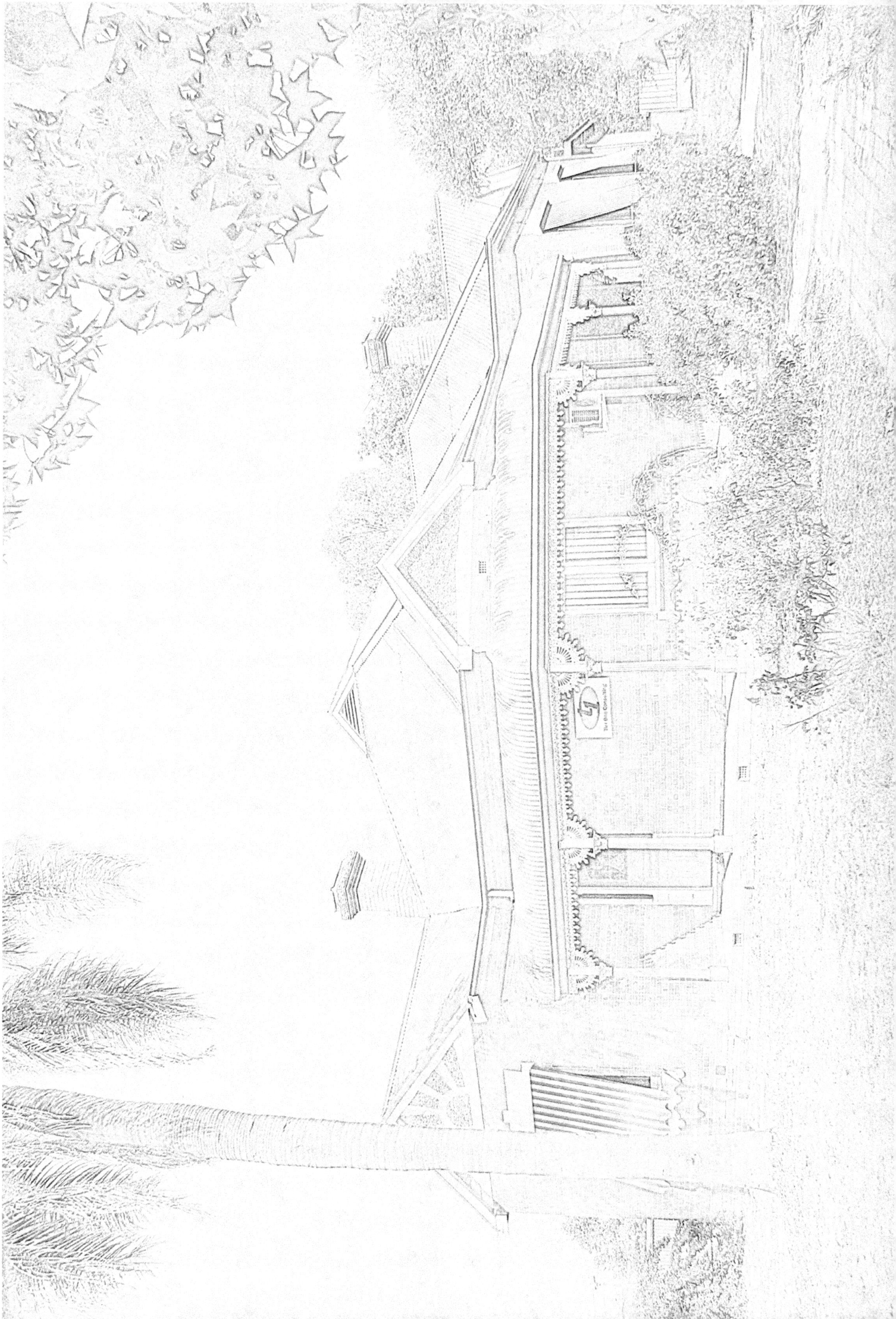

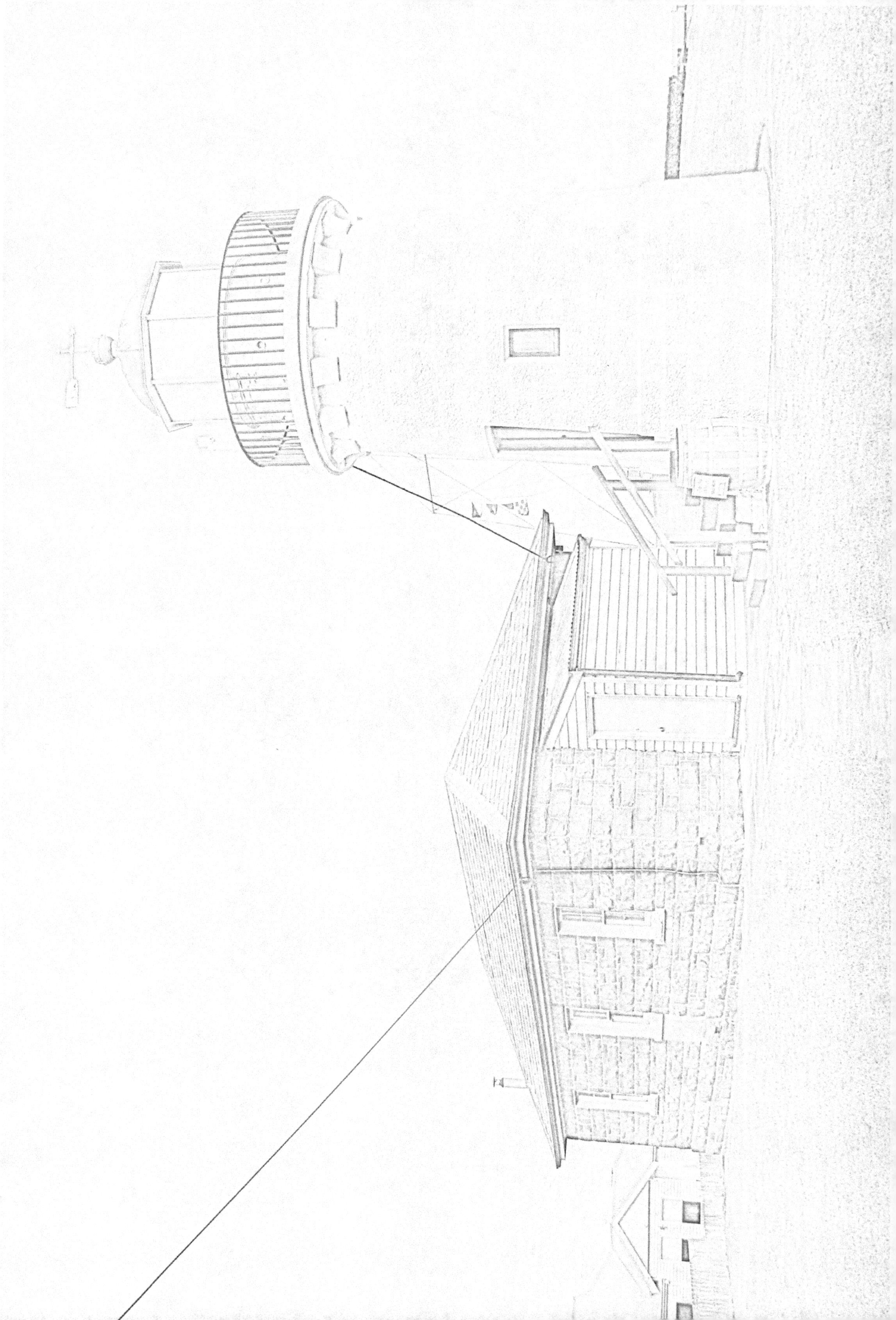

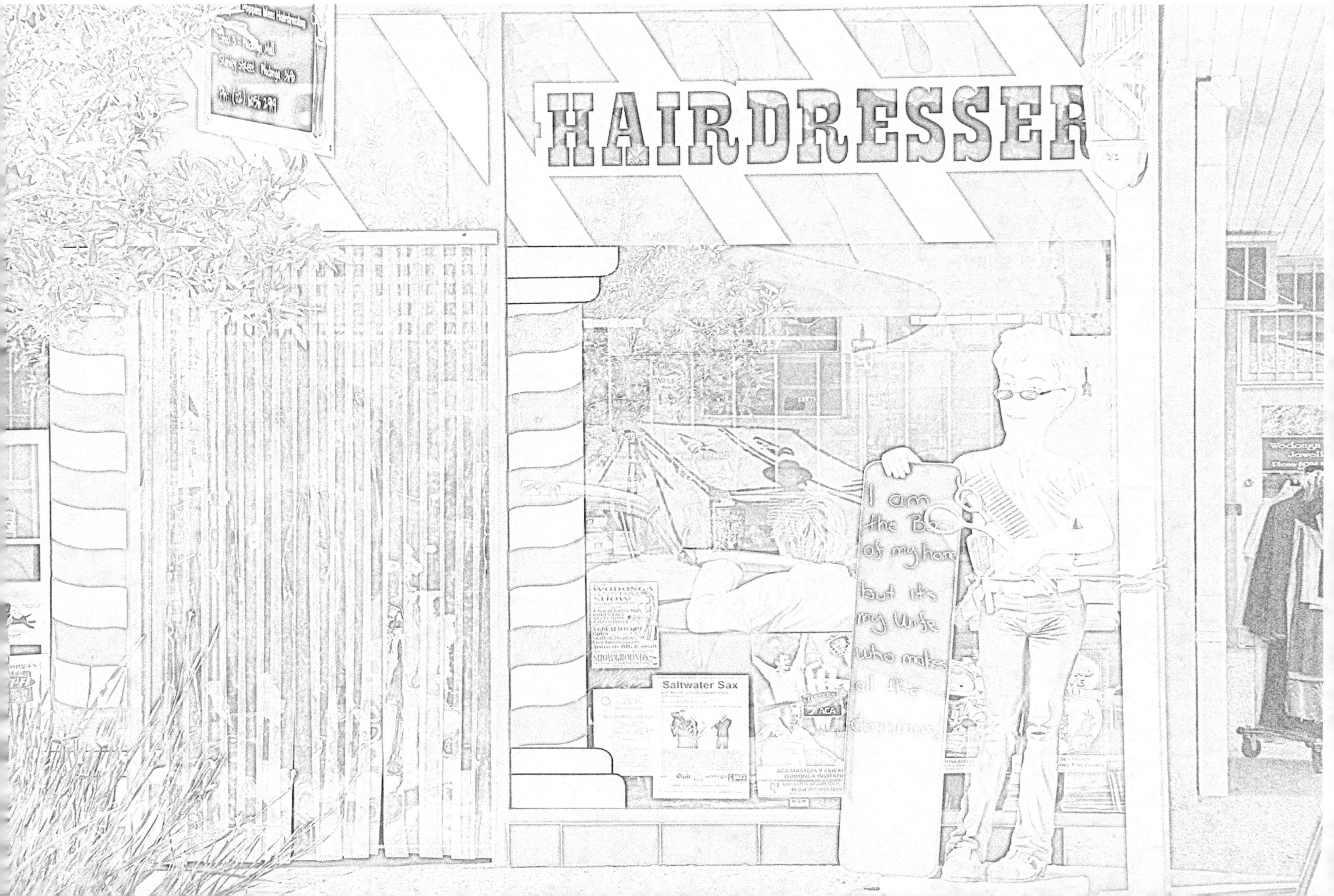
HAIRDRESSER
I am the Boss of my home but it's my Wife who makes all the decisions
Saltwater Sax
SHOWGROUNDS

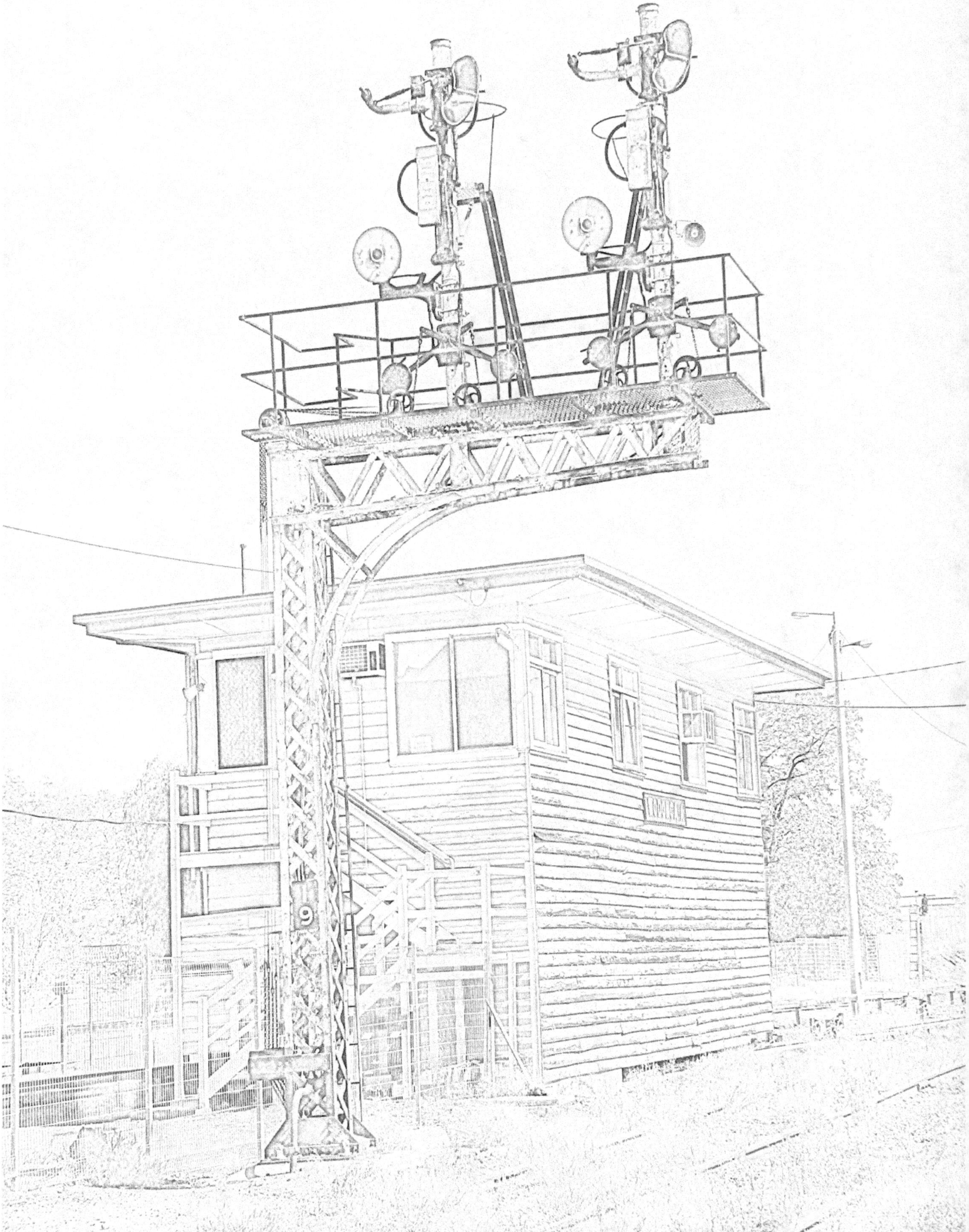
9

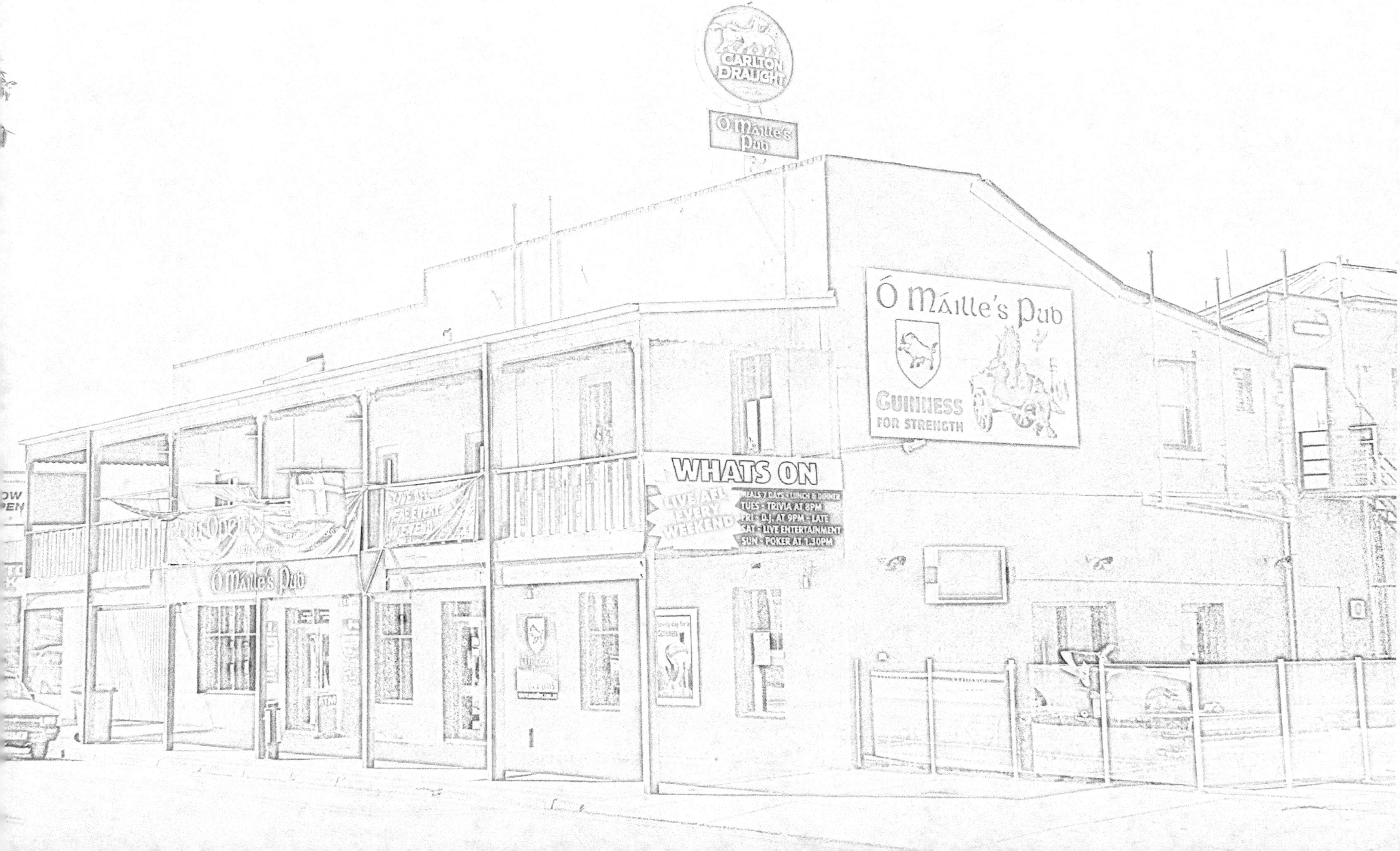
CARLTON DRAUGHT
Ó Máille's Pub
Ó Máille's Pub
GUINNESS
FOR STRENGTH
WHATS ON
LIVE AFL EVERY WEEKEND
MEALS 7 DAYS - LUNCH & DINNER
TUES - TRIVIA AT 8PM
FRI - D.J. AT 9PM - LATE
SAT - LIVE ENTERTAINMENT
SUN - POKER AT 1.30PM
Ó Máille's Pub

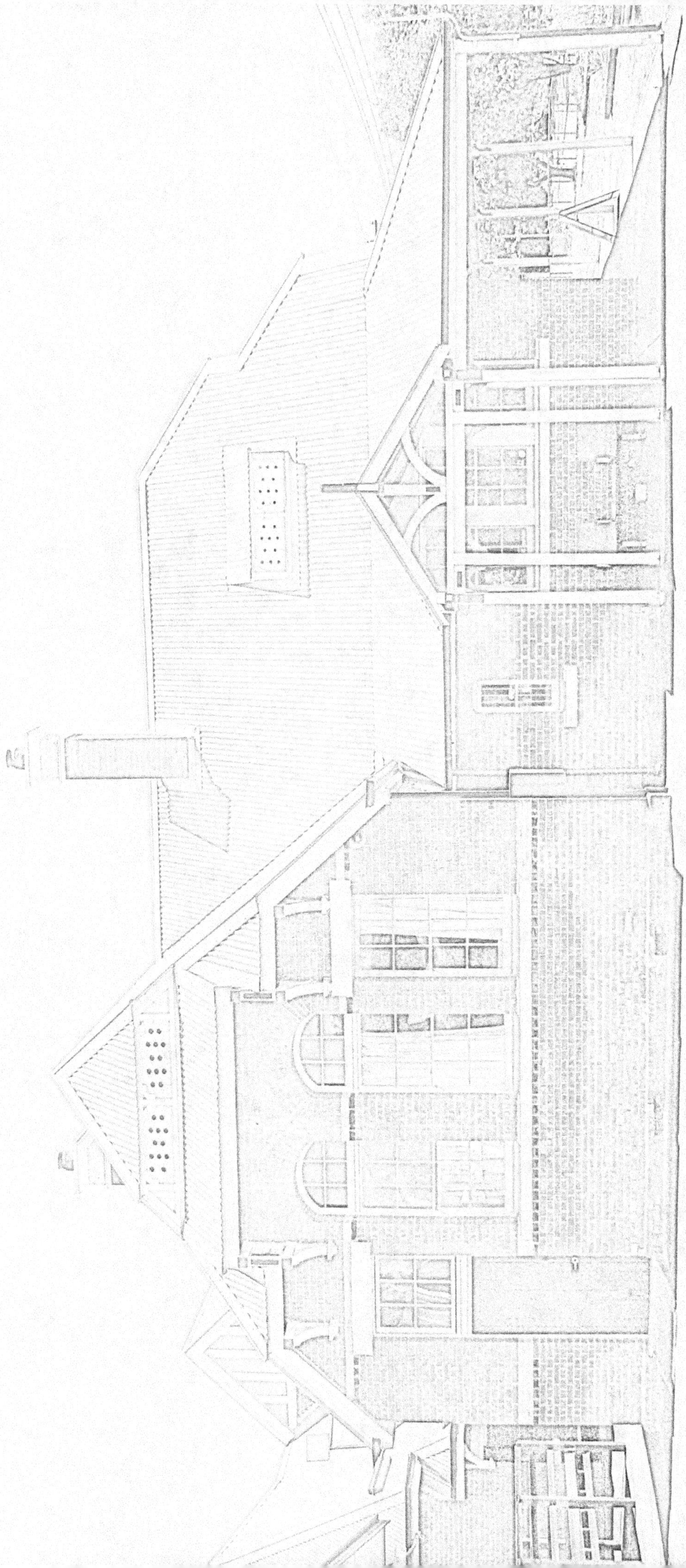

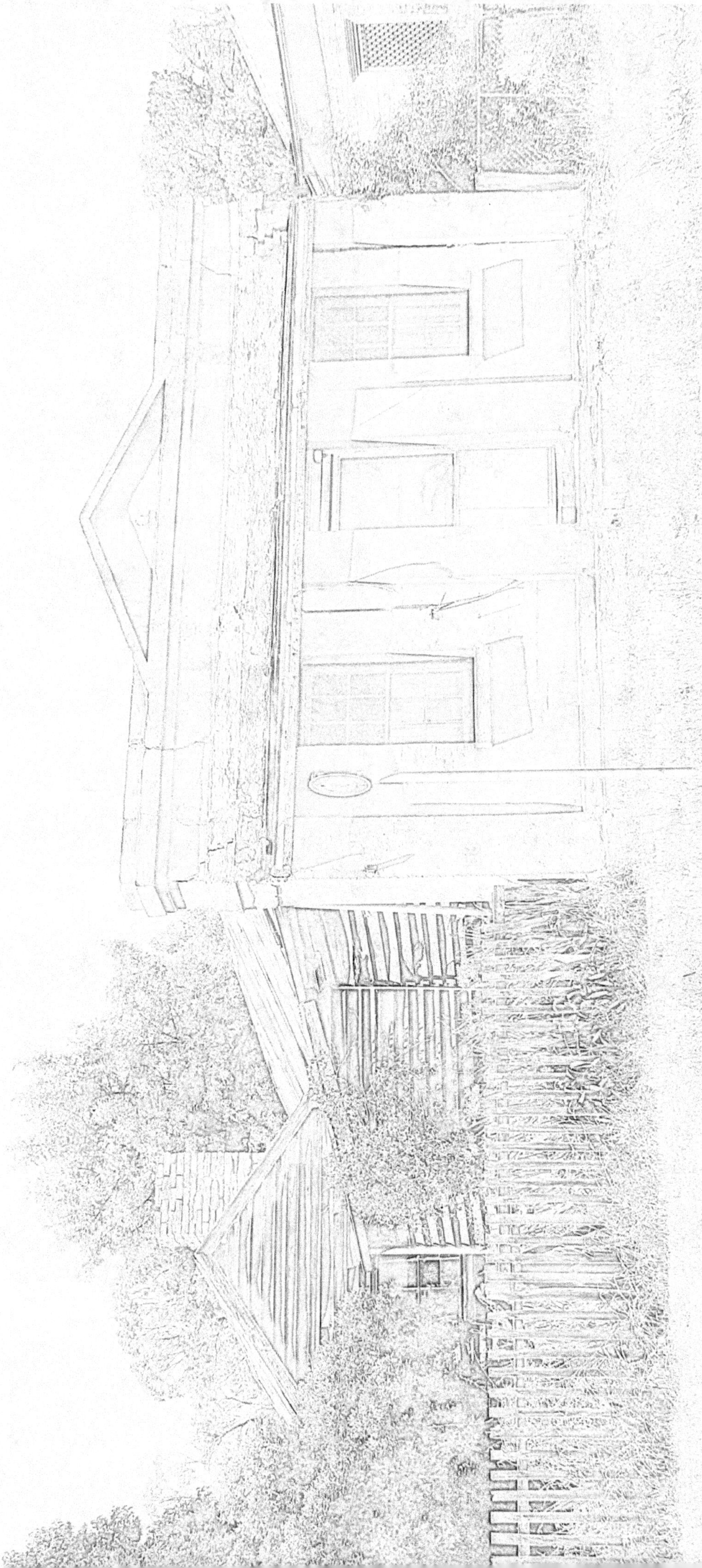

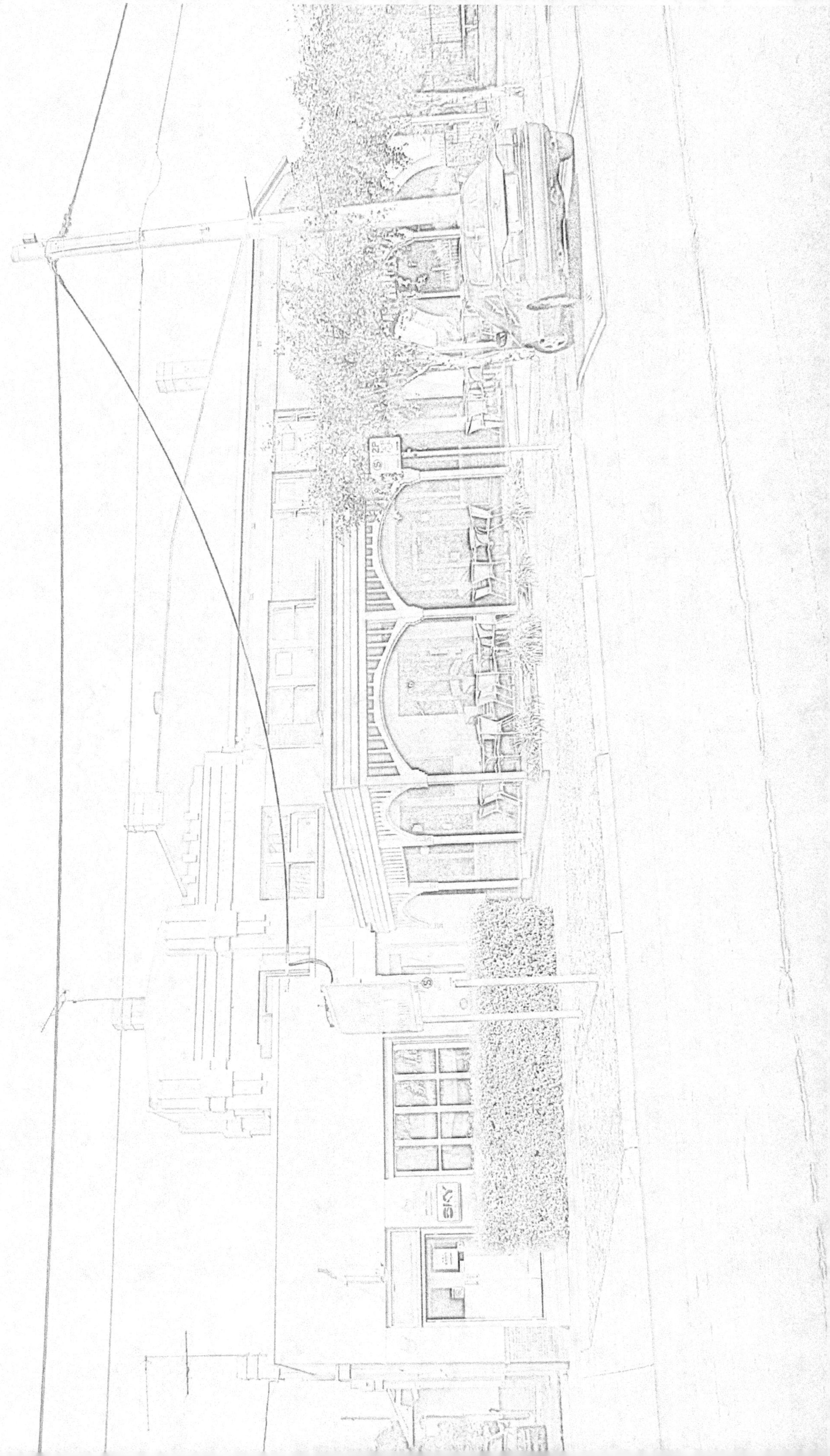

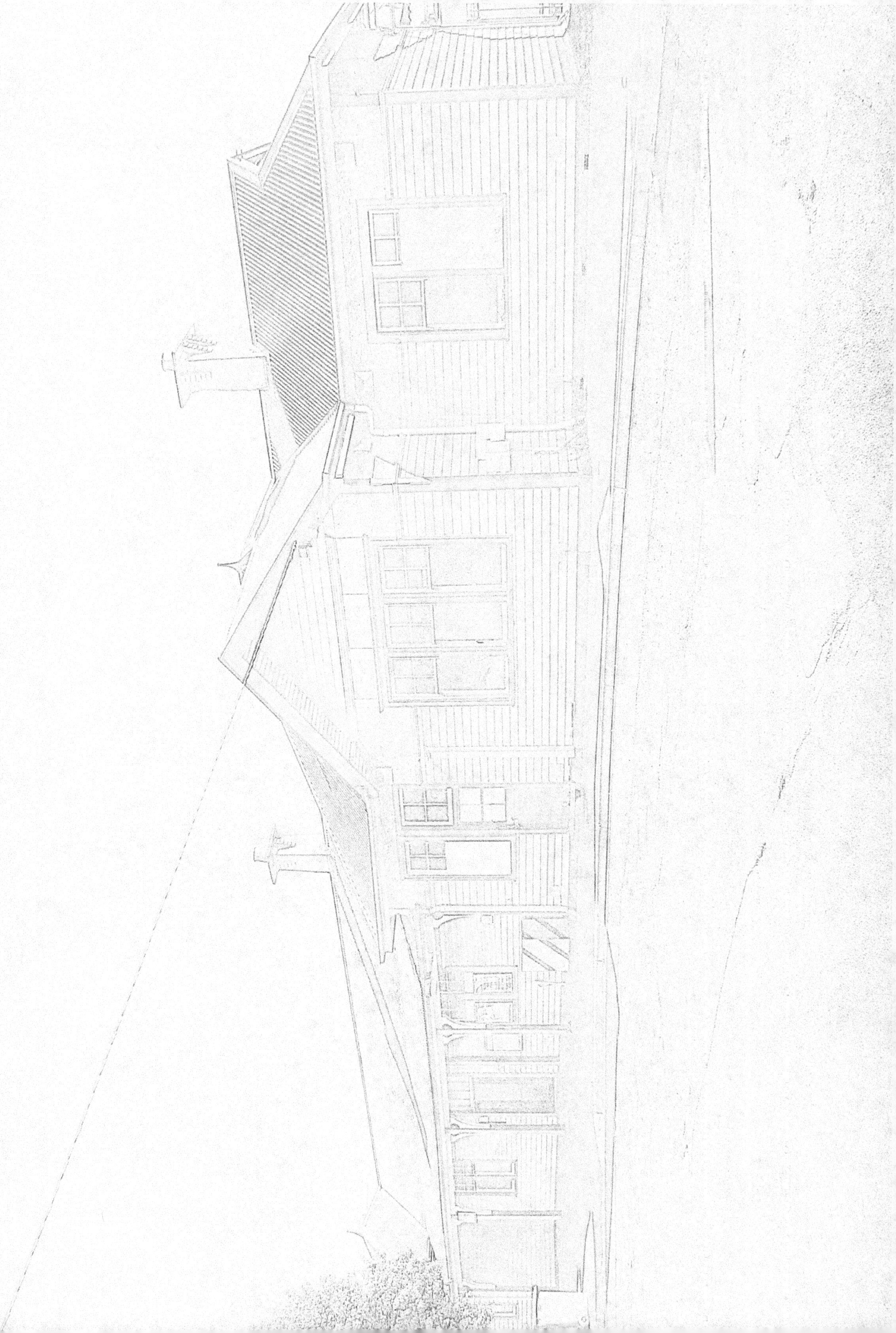

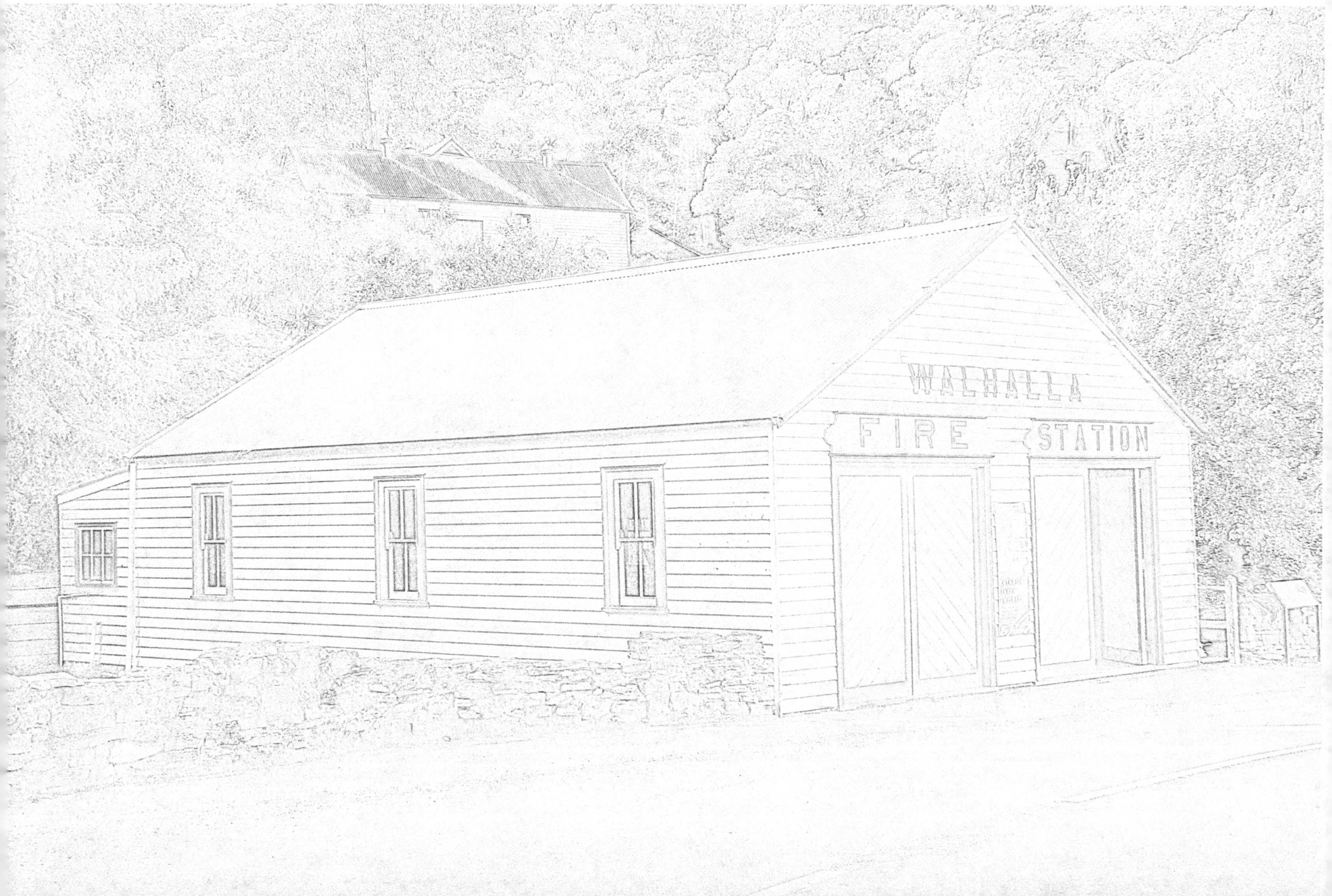
WALHALLA
FIRE STATION

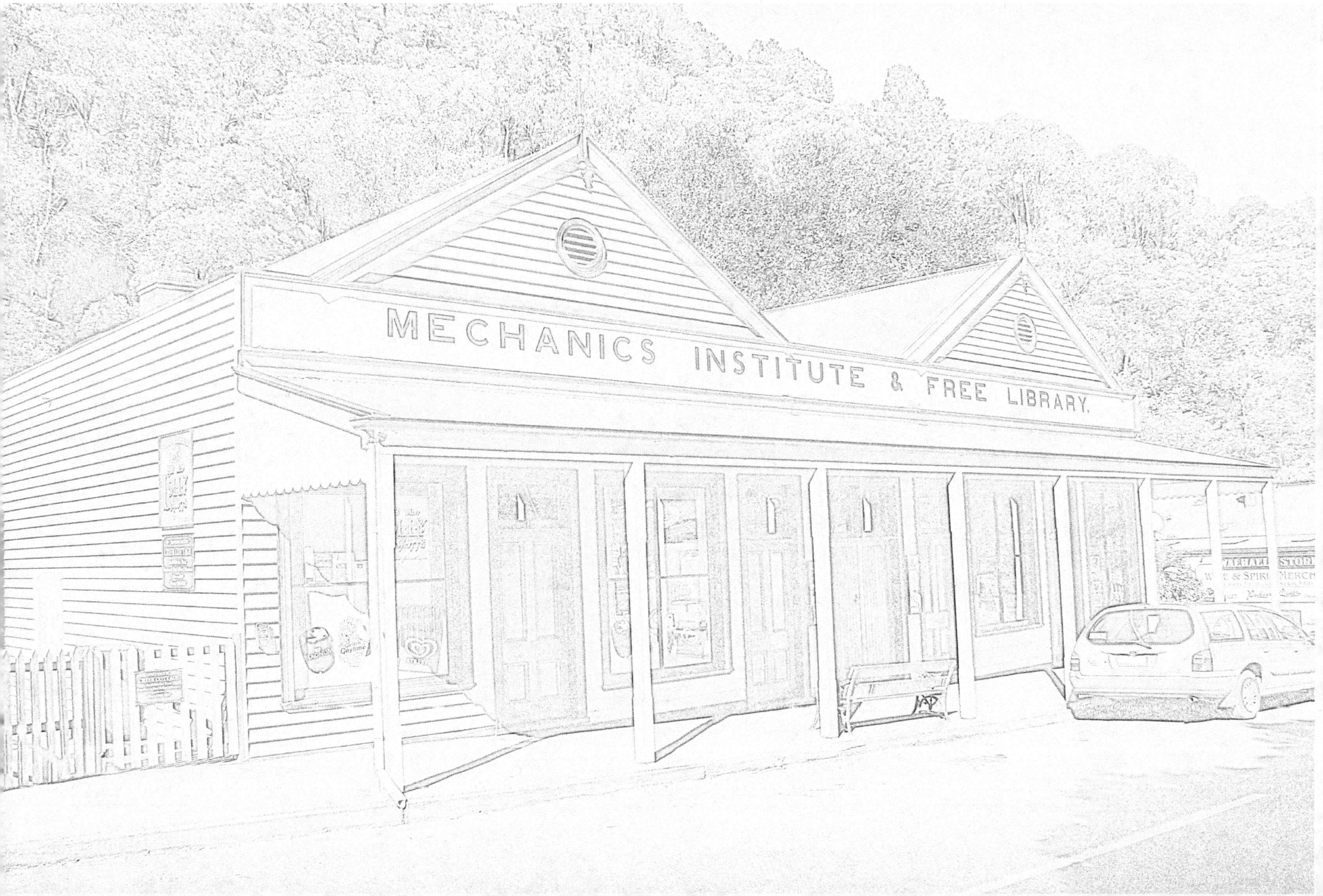
MECHANICS INSTITUTE & FREE LIBRARY.

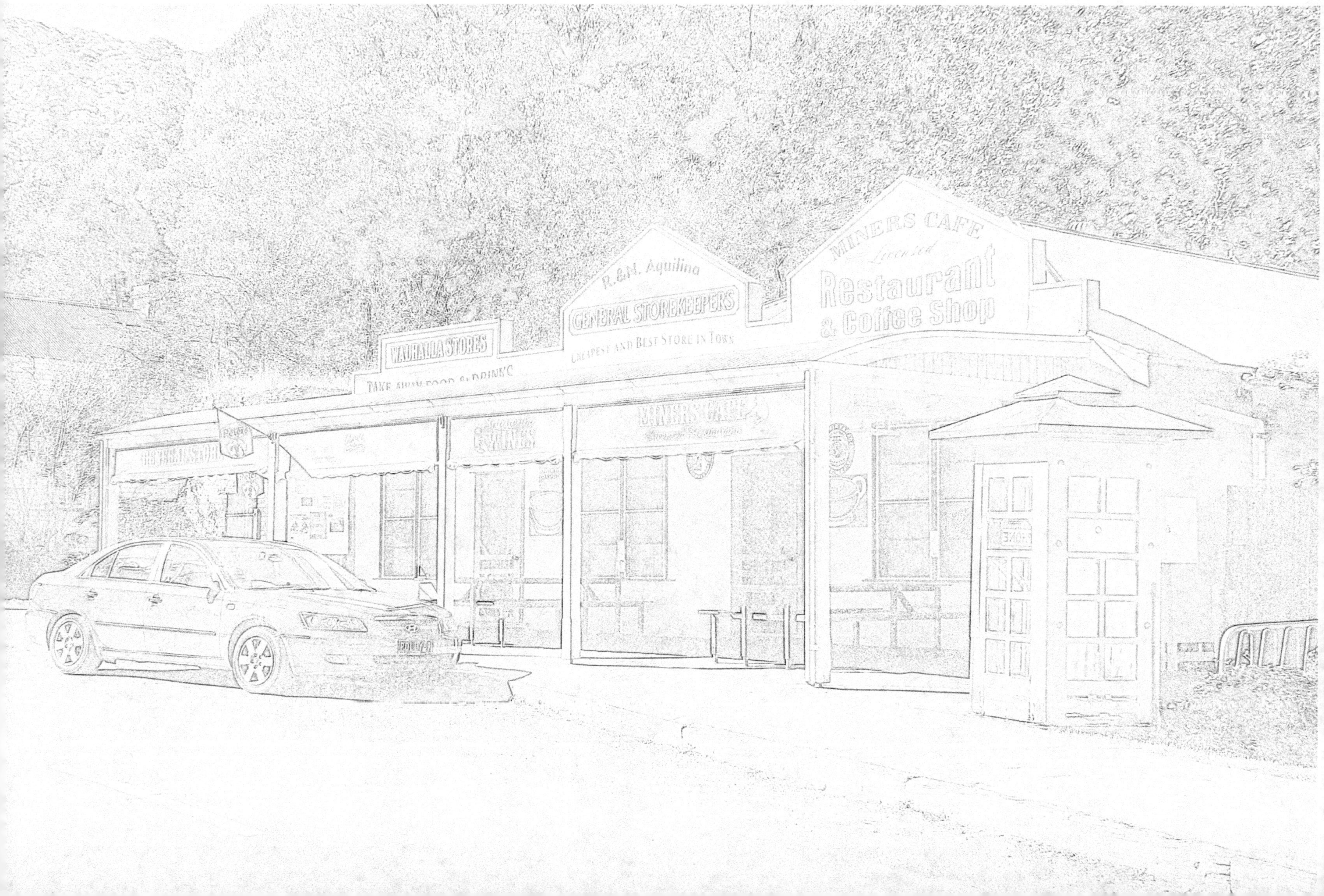
MINERS CAFE
Restaurant
& Coffee Shop
R.&N. Aquilina
GENERAL STOREKEEPERS
CHEAPEST AND BEST STORE IN TOWN
WALHALLA STORES
MINERS CAFE

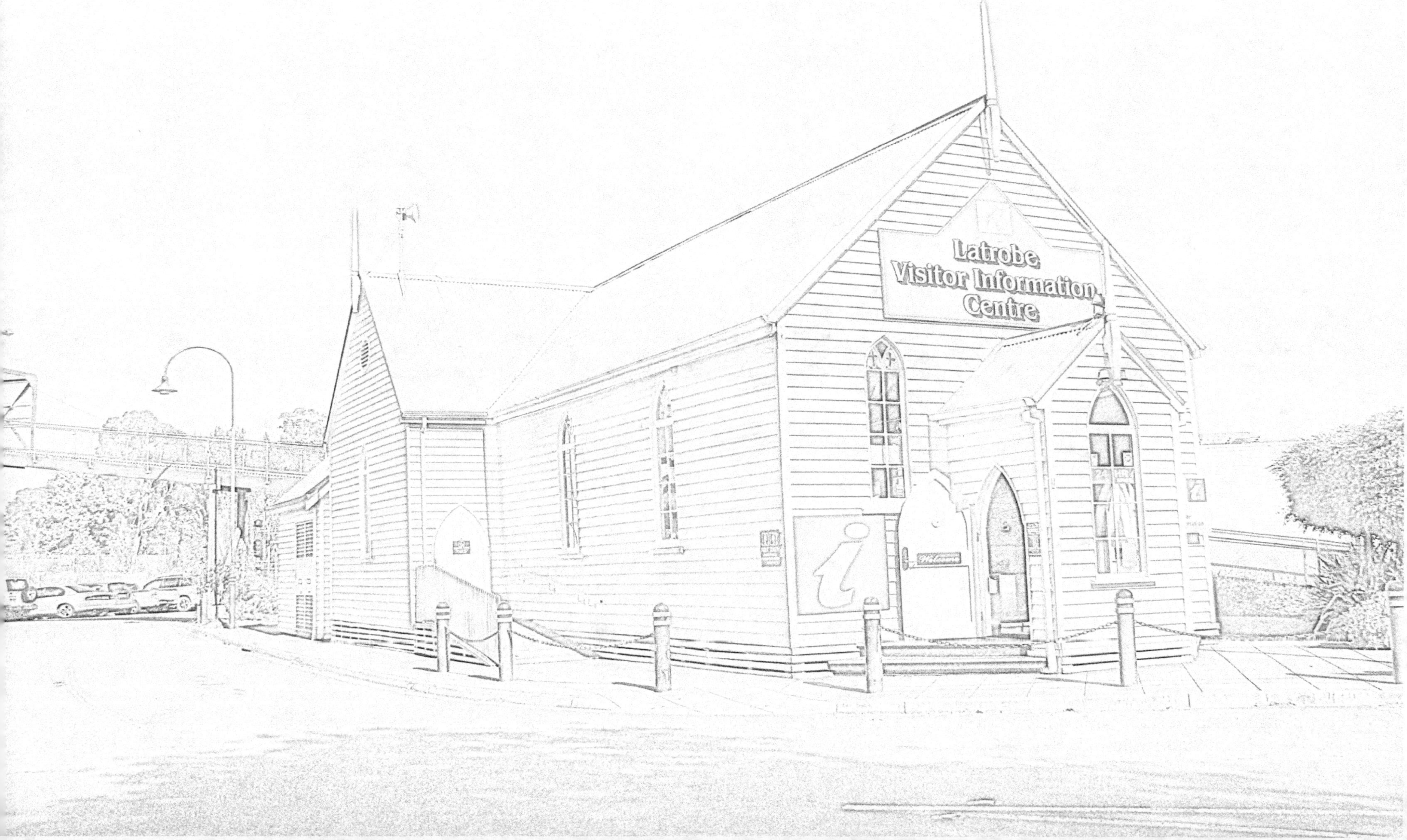
Latrobe
Visitor Information
Centre

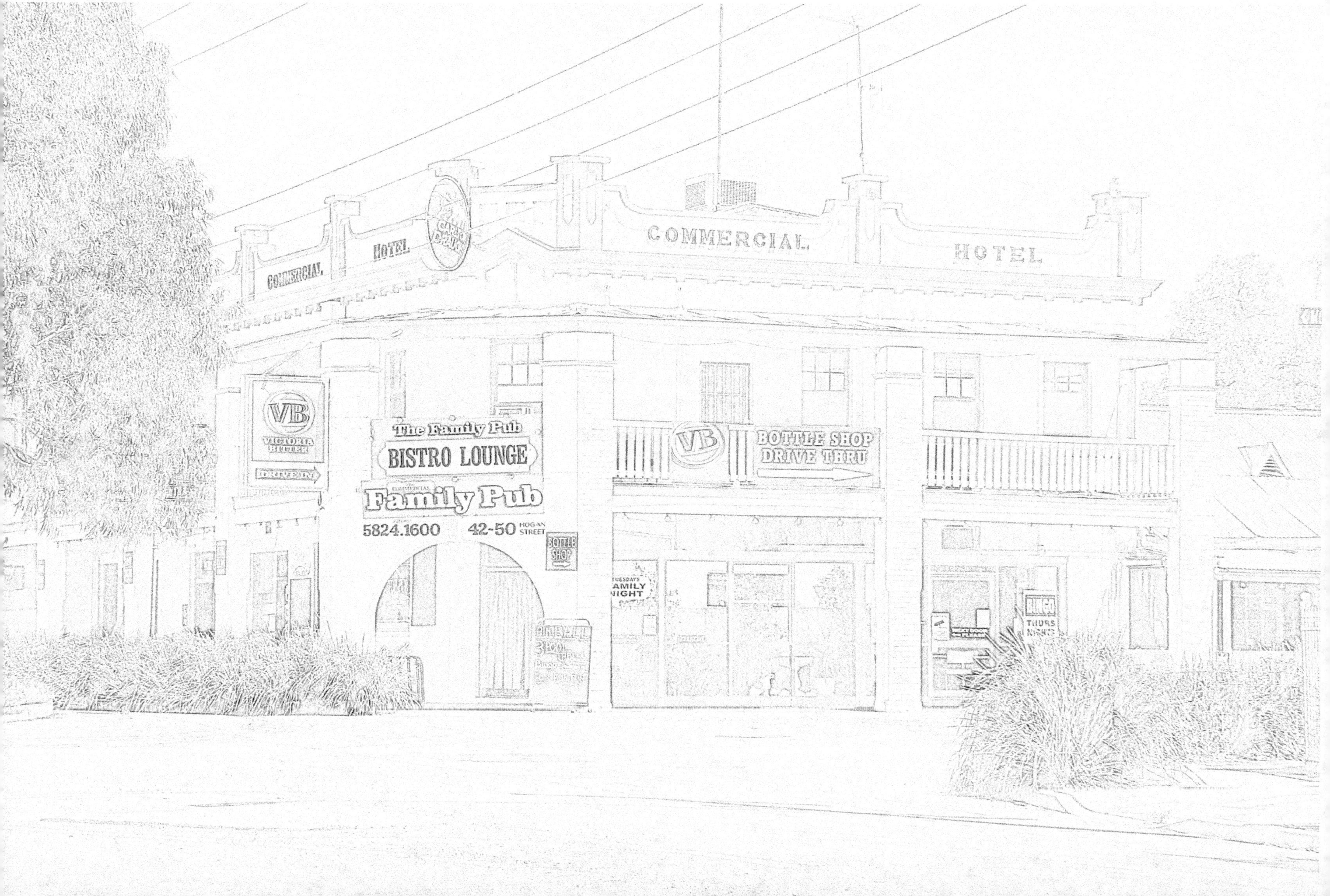
COMMERCIAL HOTEL
COMMERCIAL HOTEL
VB
VICTORIA BITTER
DRIVE IN
The Family Pub
BISTRO LOUNGE
Family Pub
5824.1600
42-50 HOGAN STREET
BOTTLE SHOP
VB
BOTTLE SHOP DRIVE THRU
TUESDAYS FAMILY NIGHT
BINGO THURS NIGHT

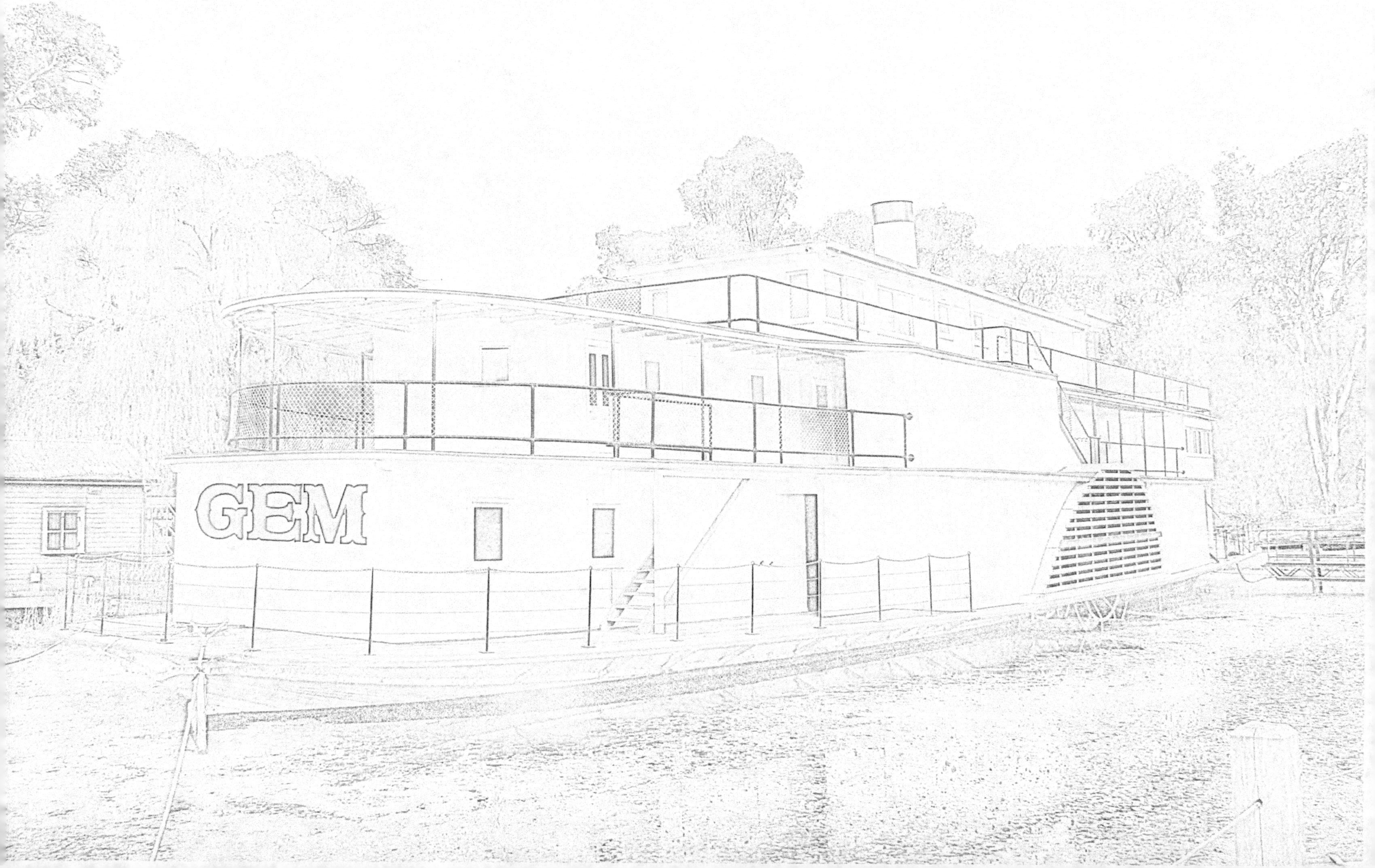
GEM

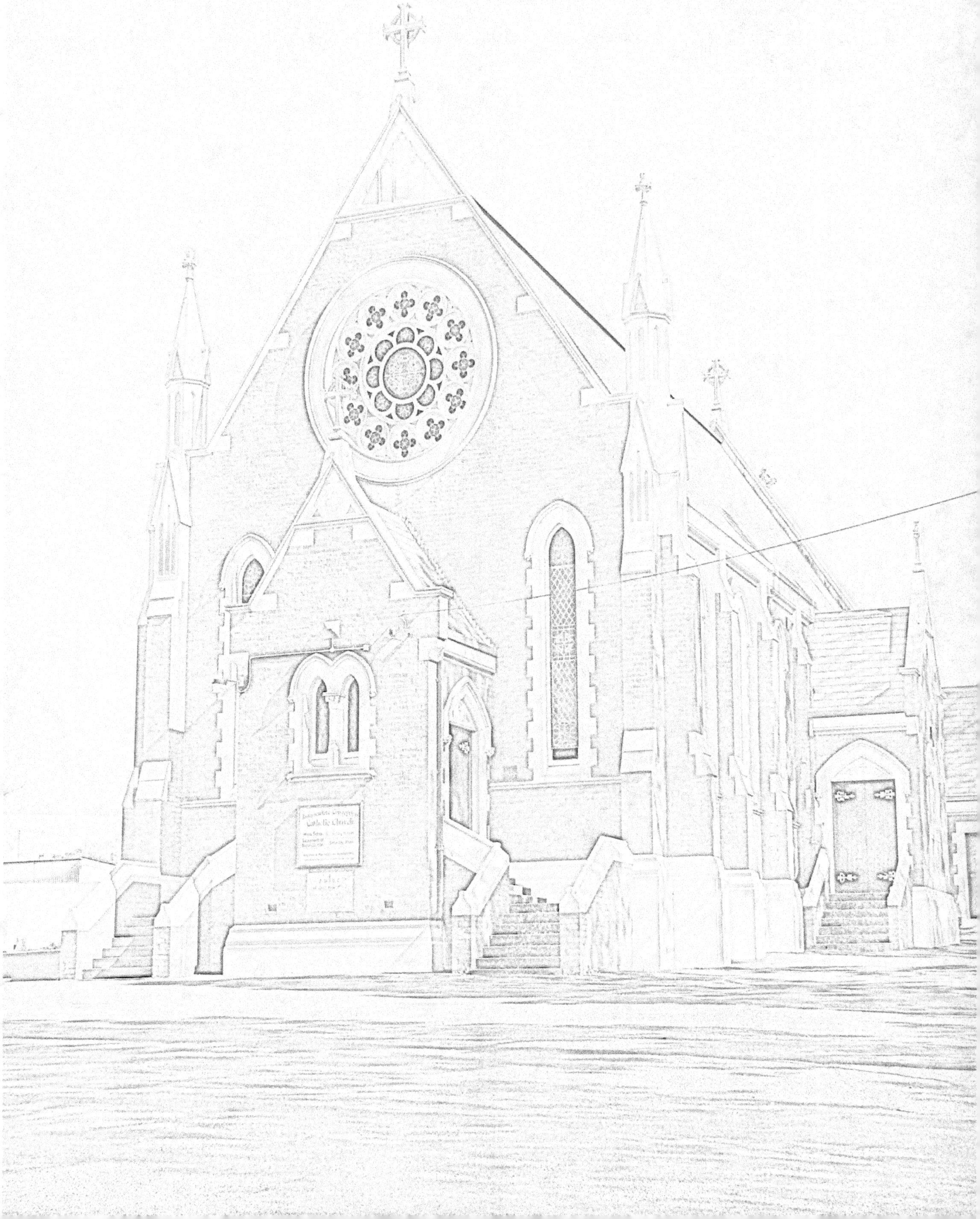
Catholic Church

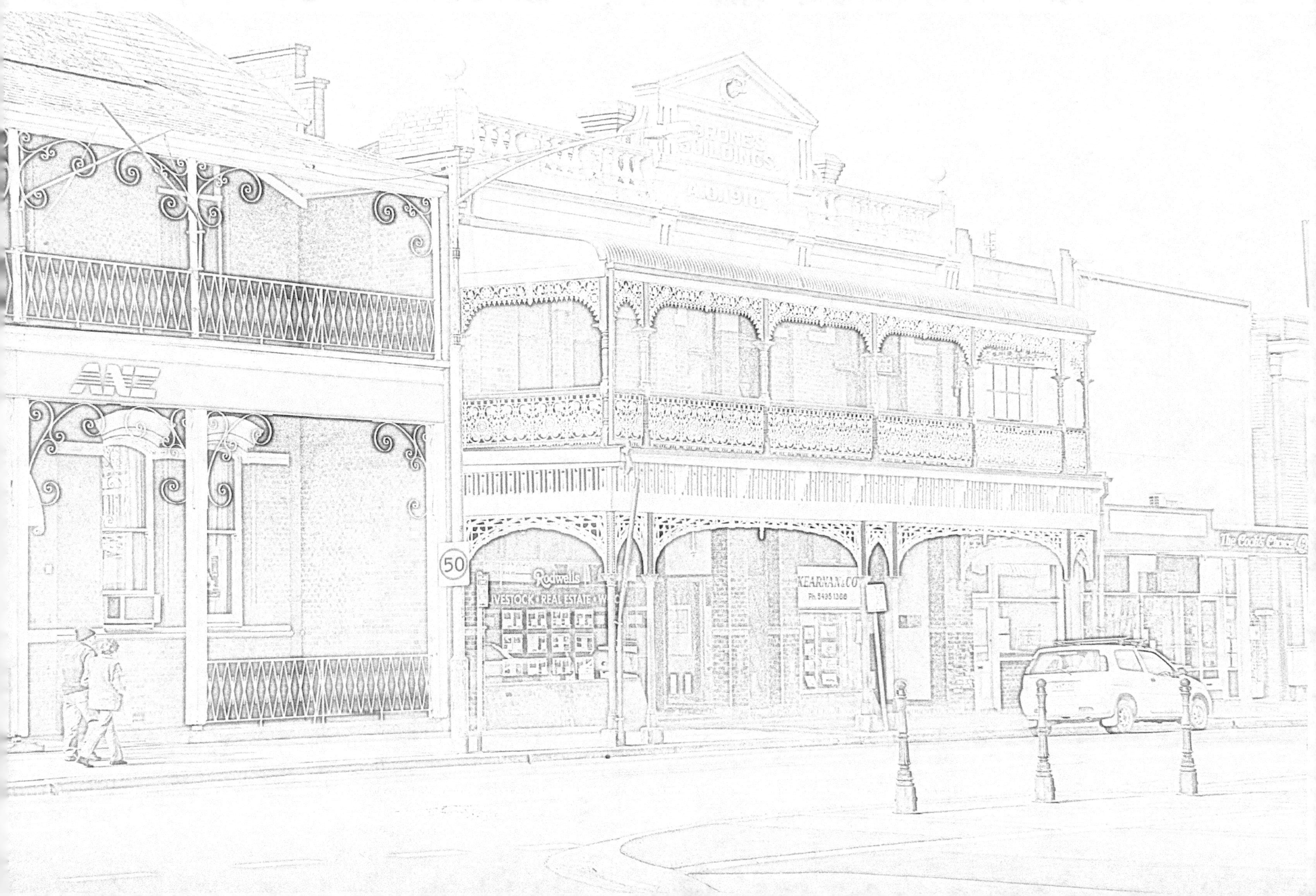

ANZ
AD 1910
50
Rodwells
LIVESTOCK • REAL ESTATE • W
KEARNAN & CO
Ph 5495 1366

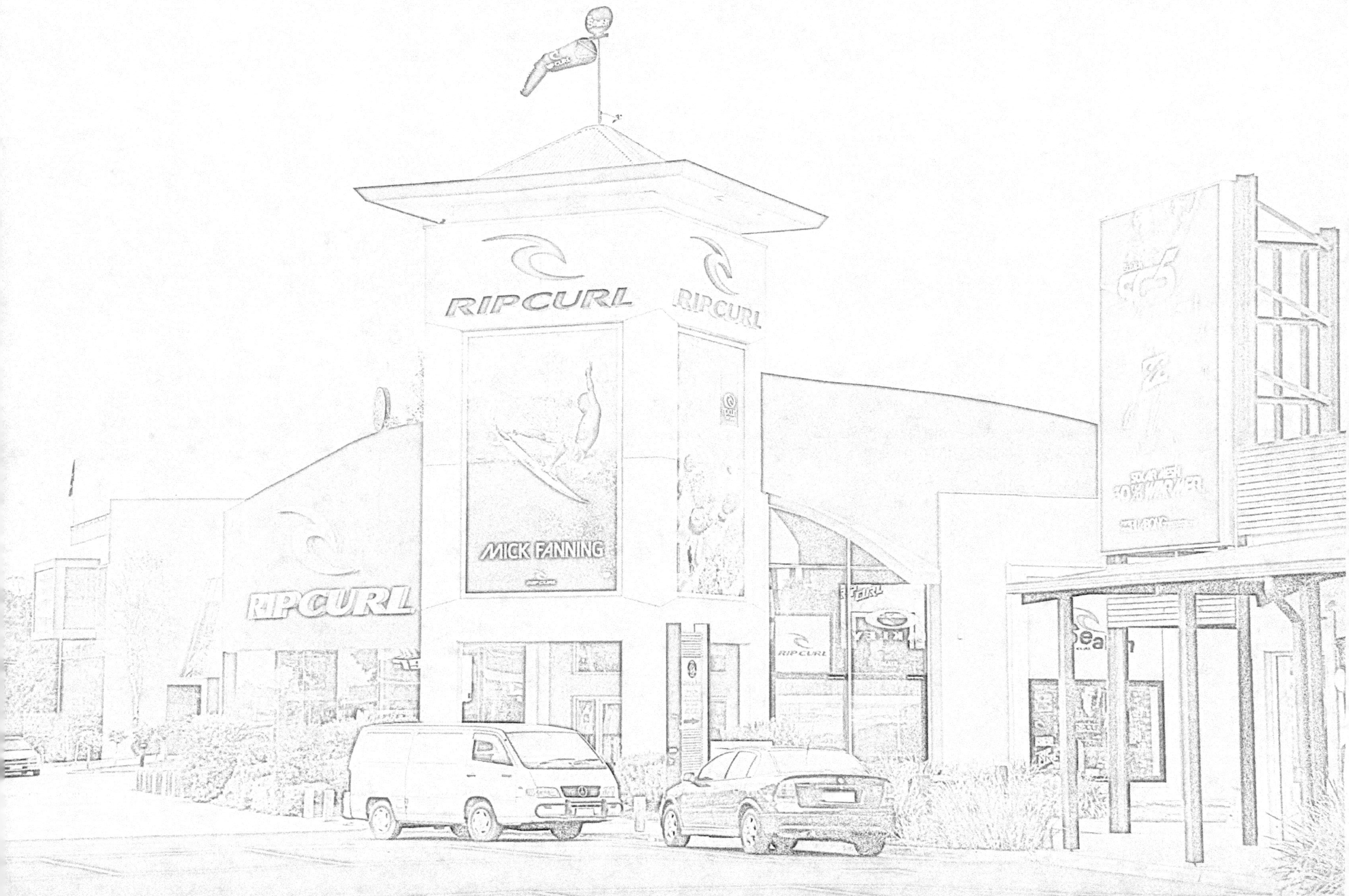
RIPCURL
RIPCURL
MICK FANNING
RIPCURL
RIP CURL

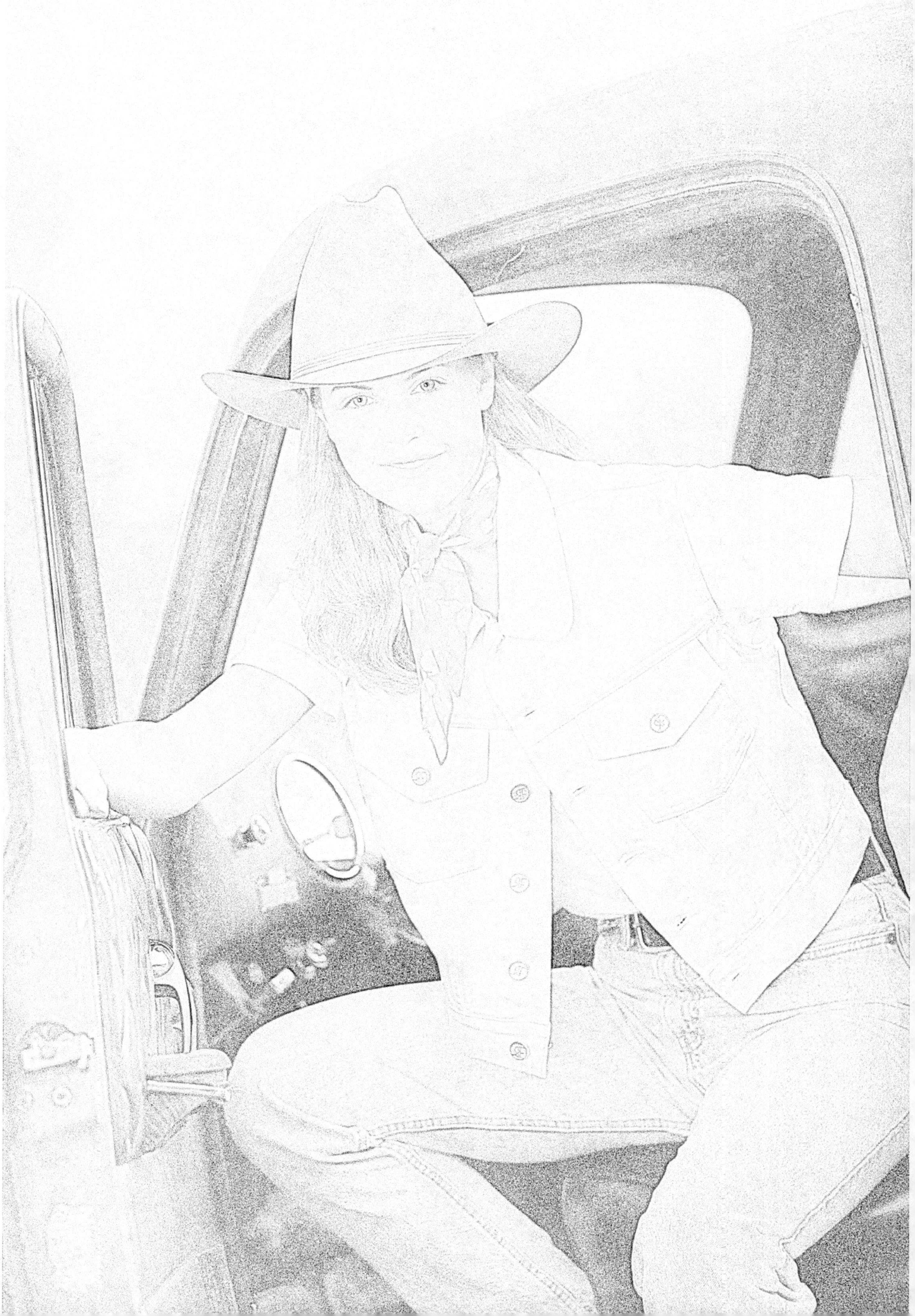

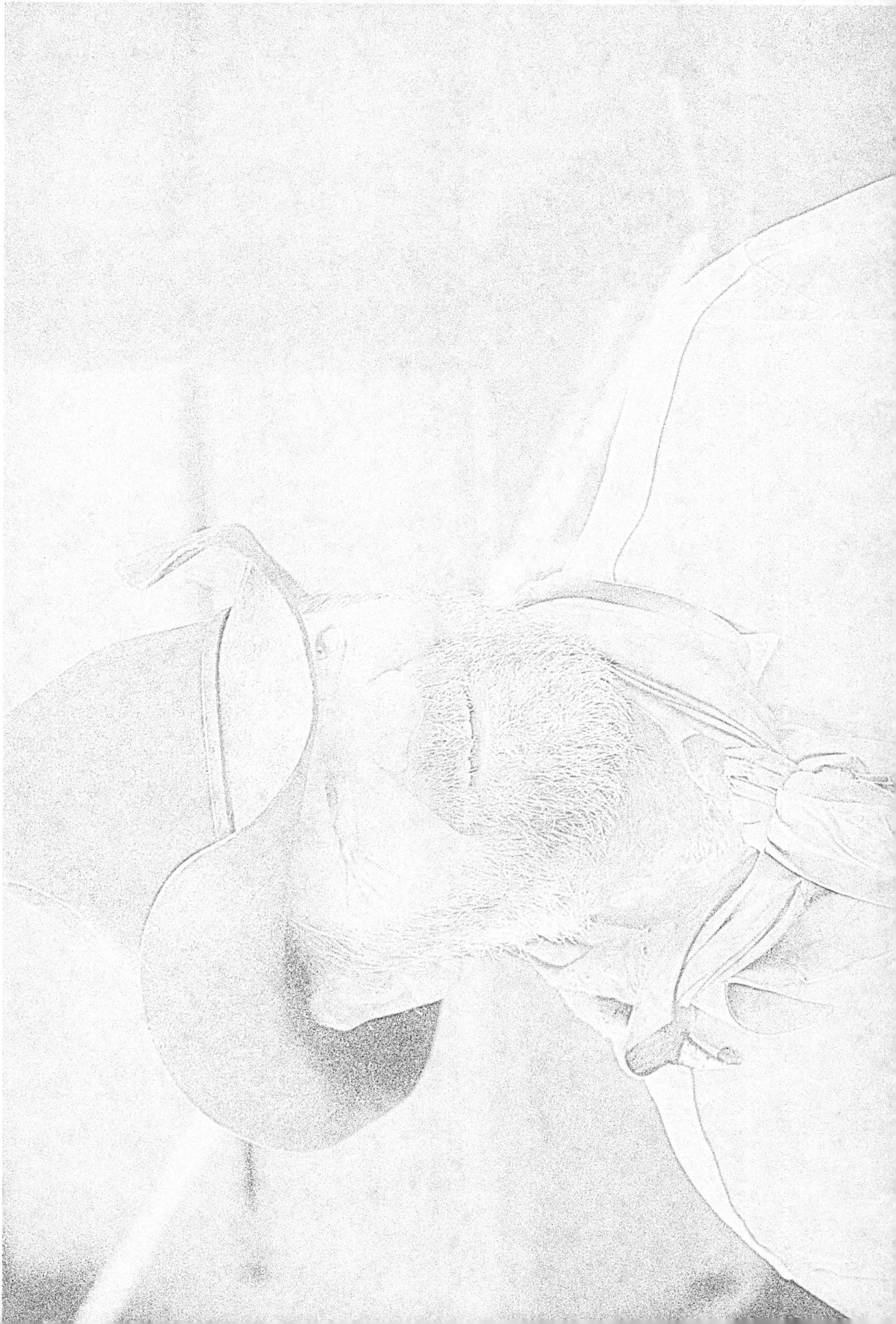

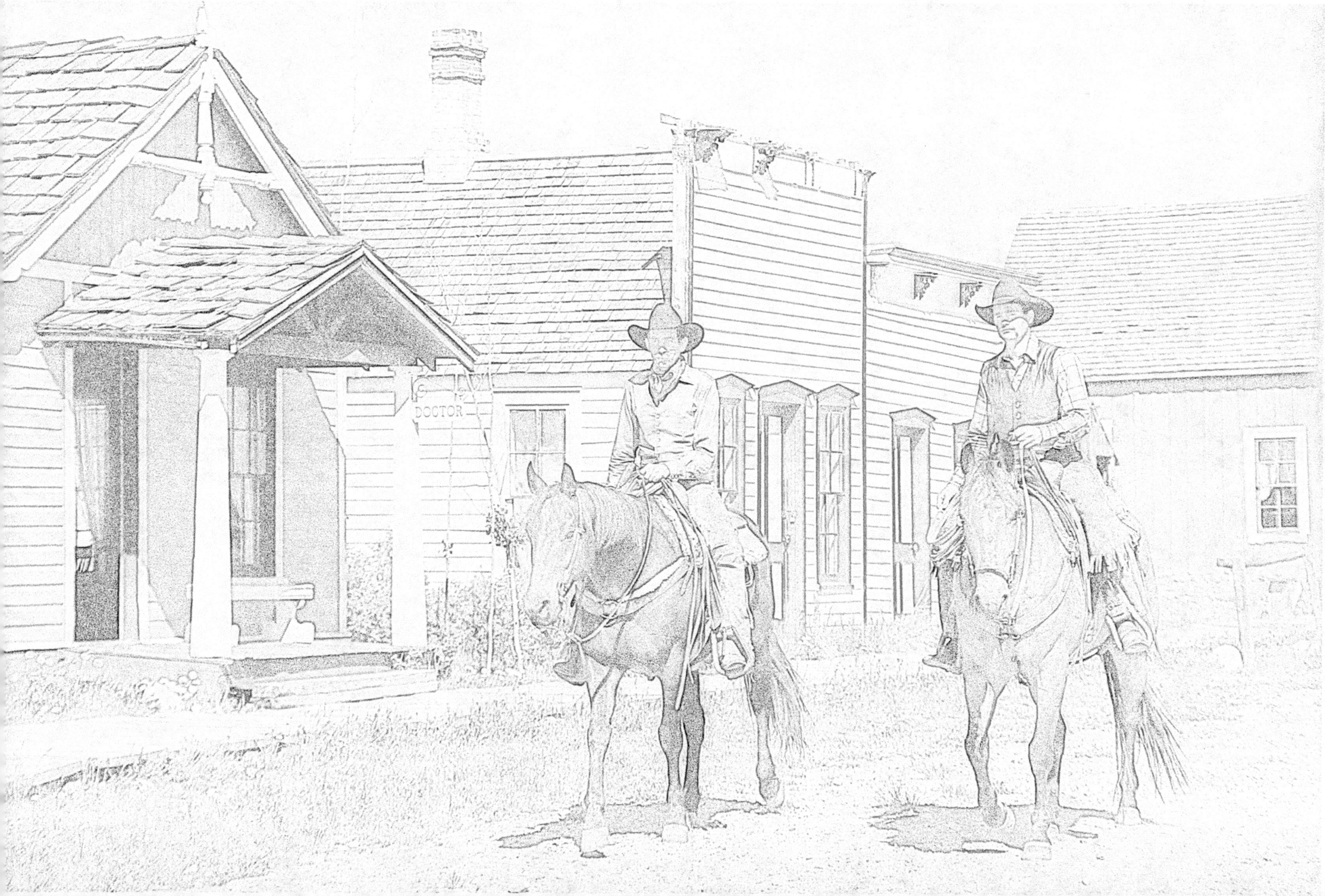
DOCTOR

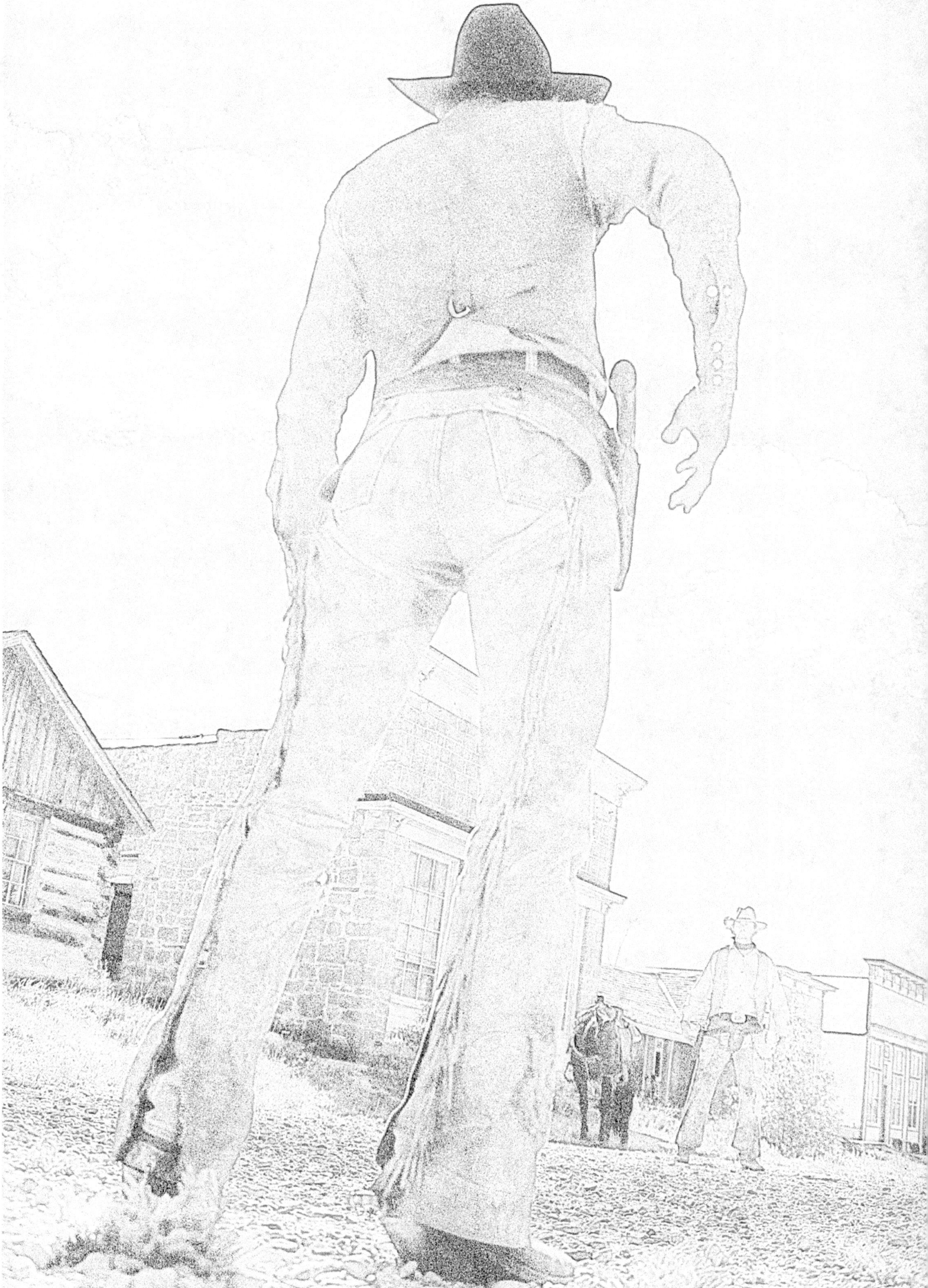

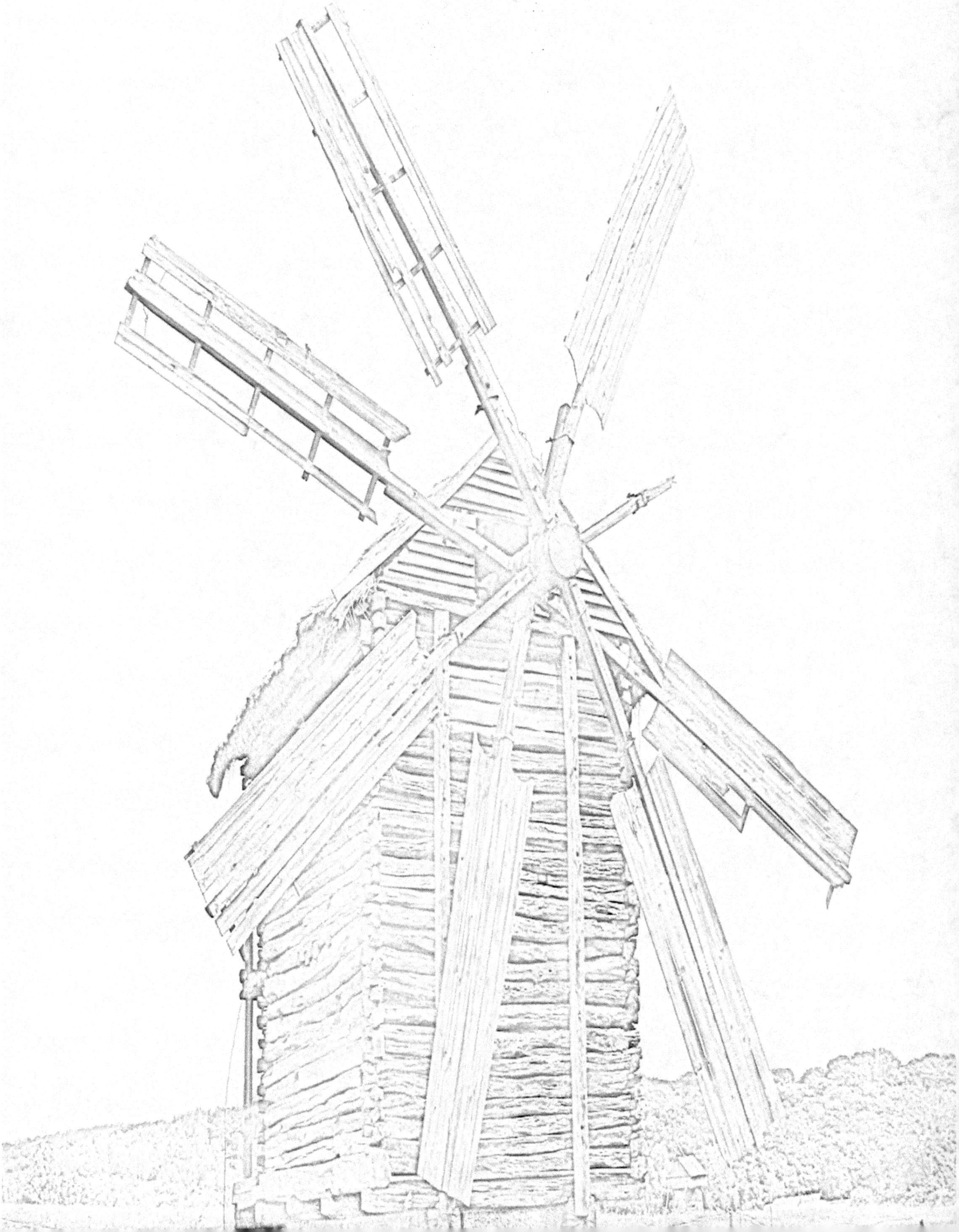

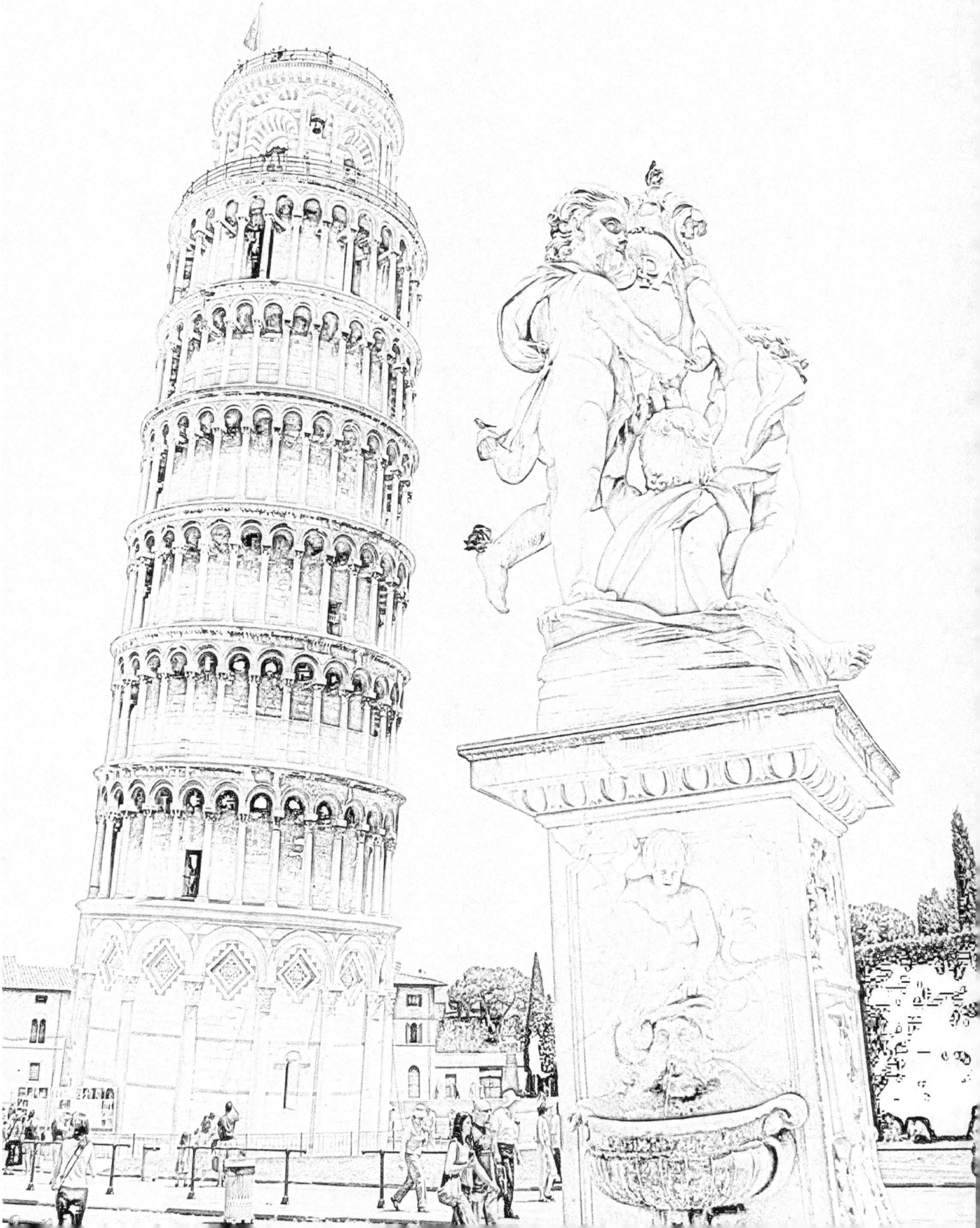

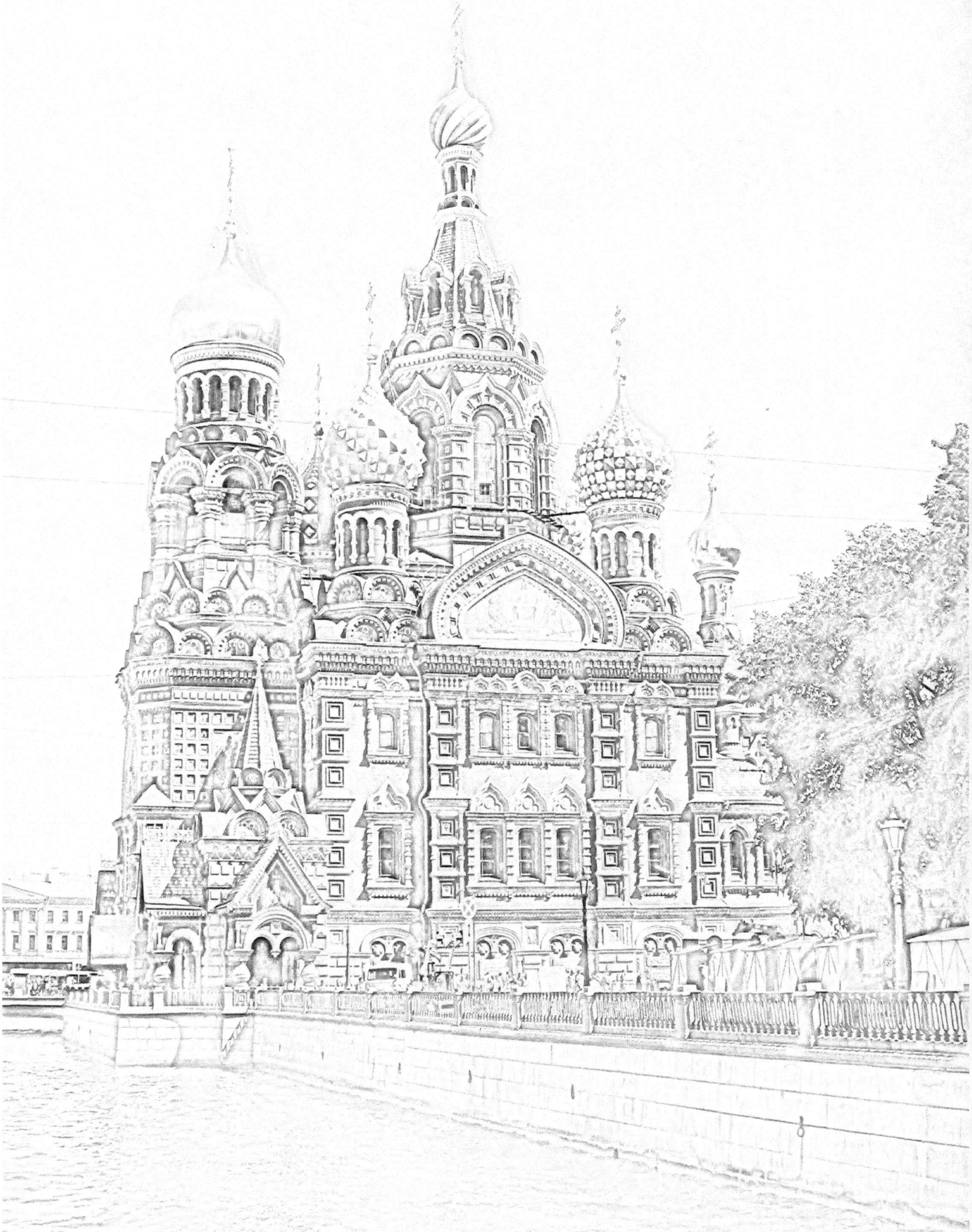

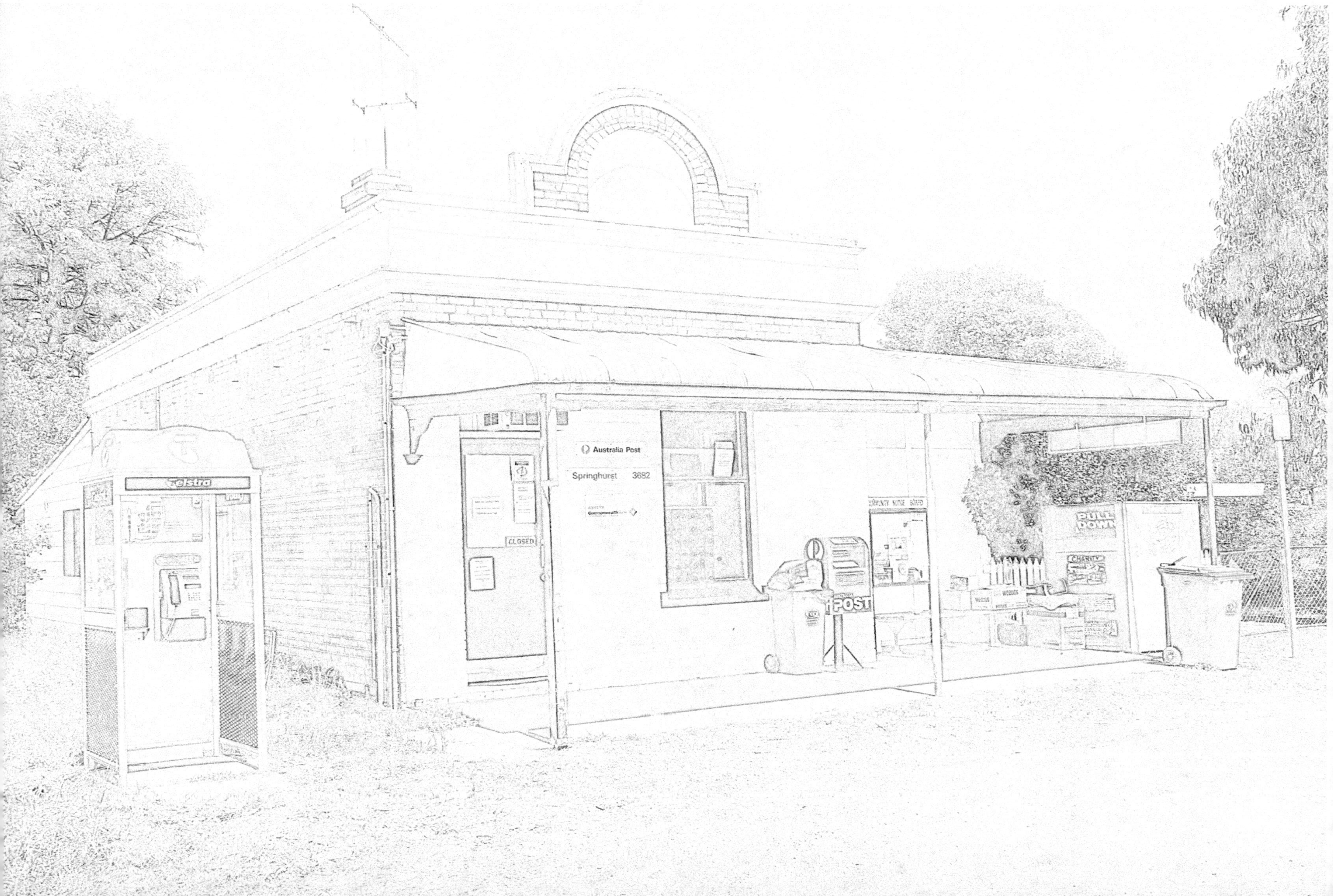
Telstra
Australia Post
Springhurst 3682
CLOSED
POST
PULL DOWN

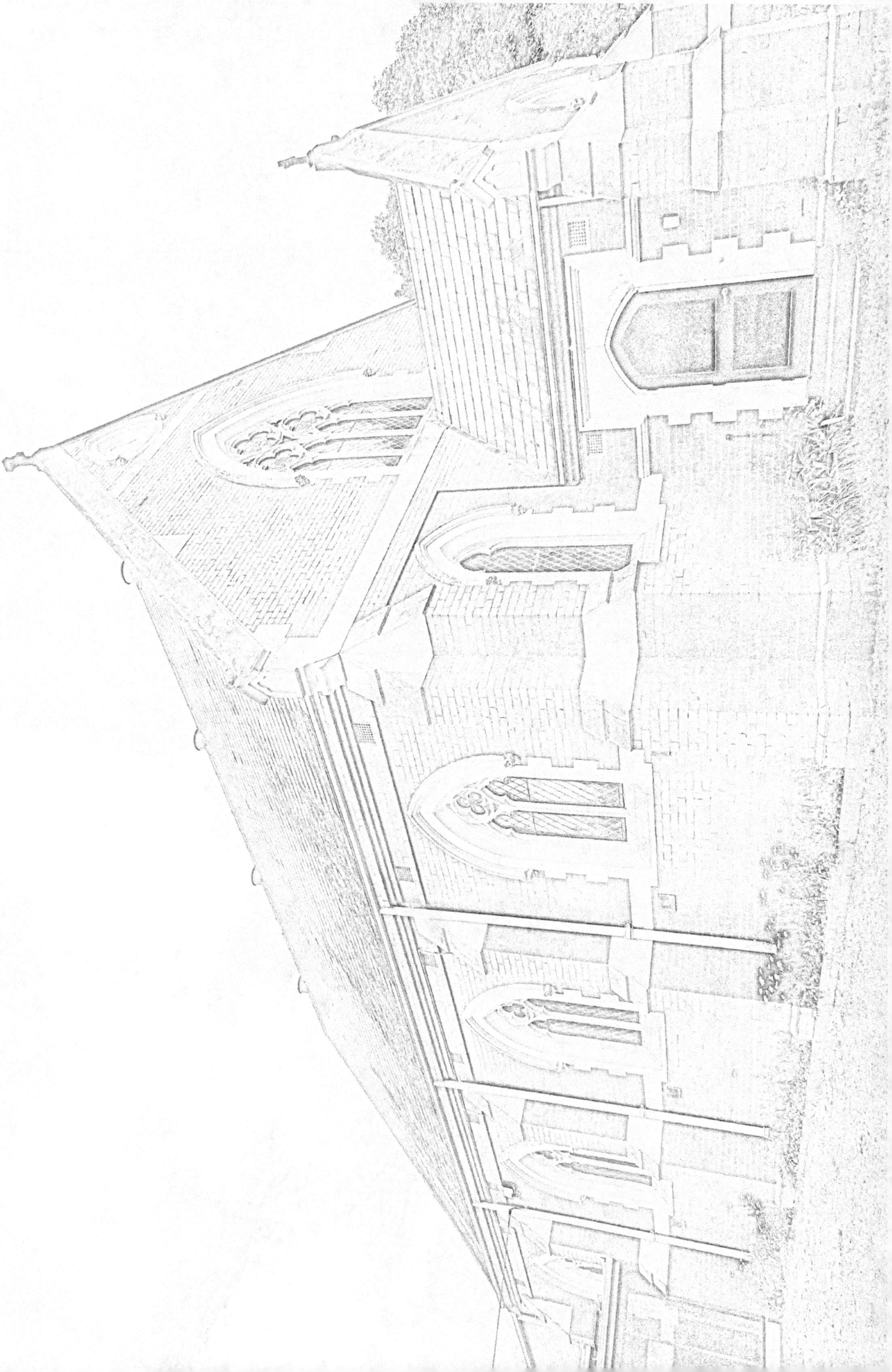

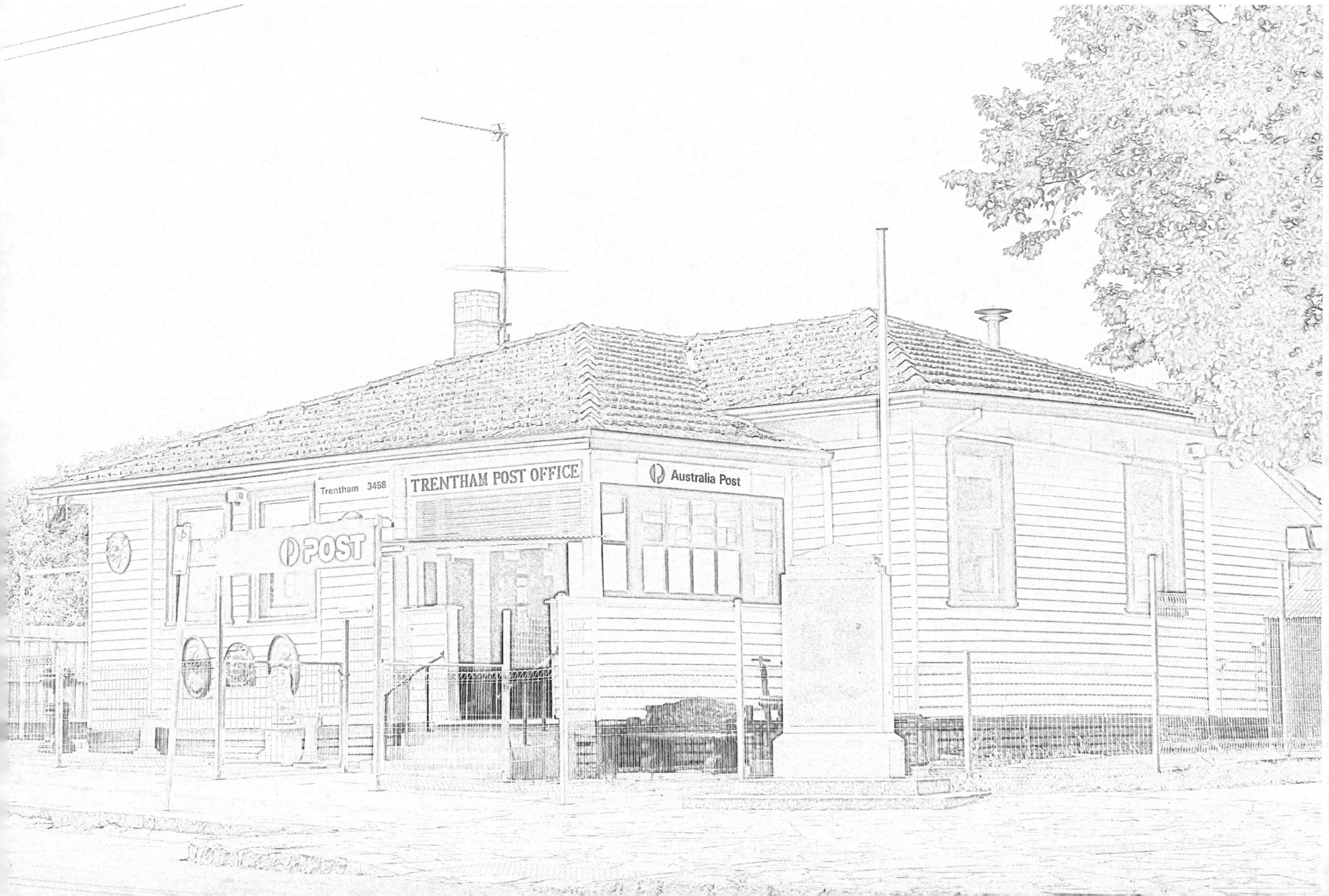

Trentham 3458
TRENTHAM POST OFFICE
Australia Post
POST

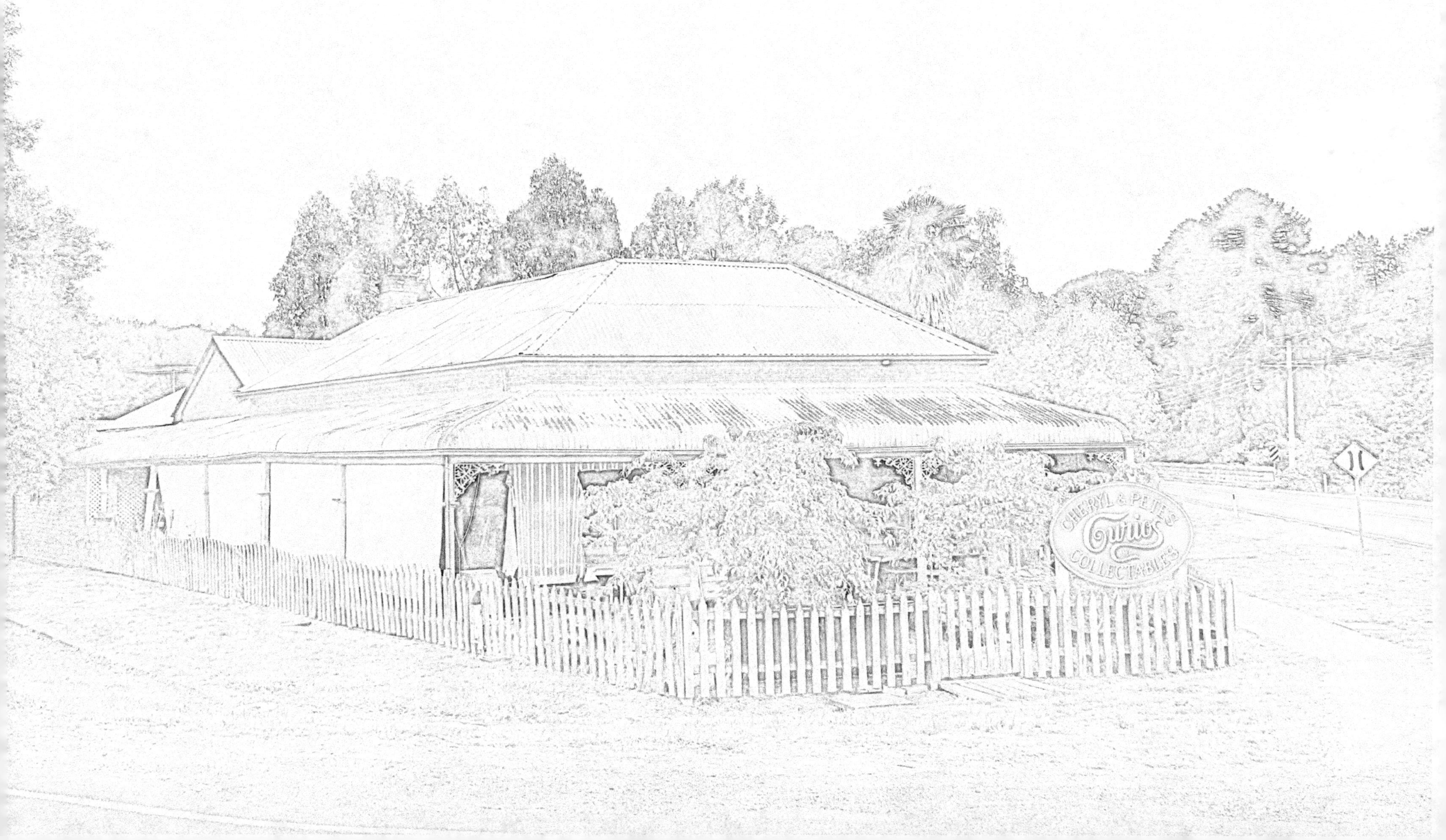
CHERYL & PETE'S
Curios
COLLECTABLES

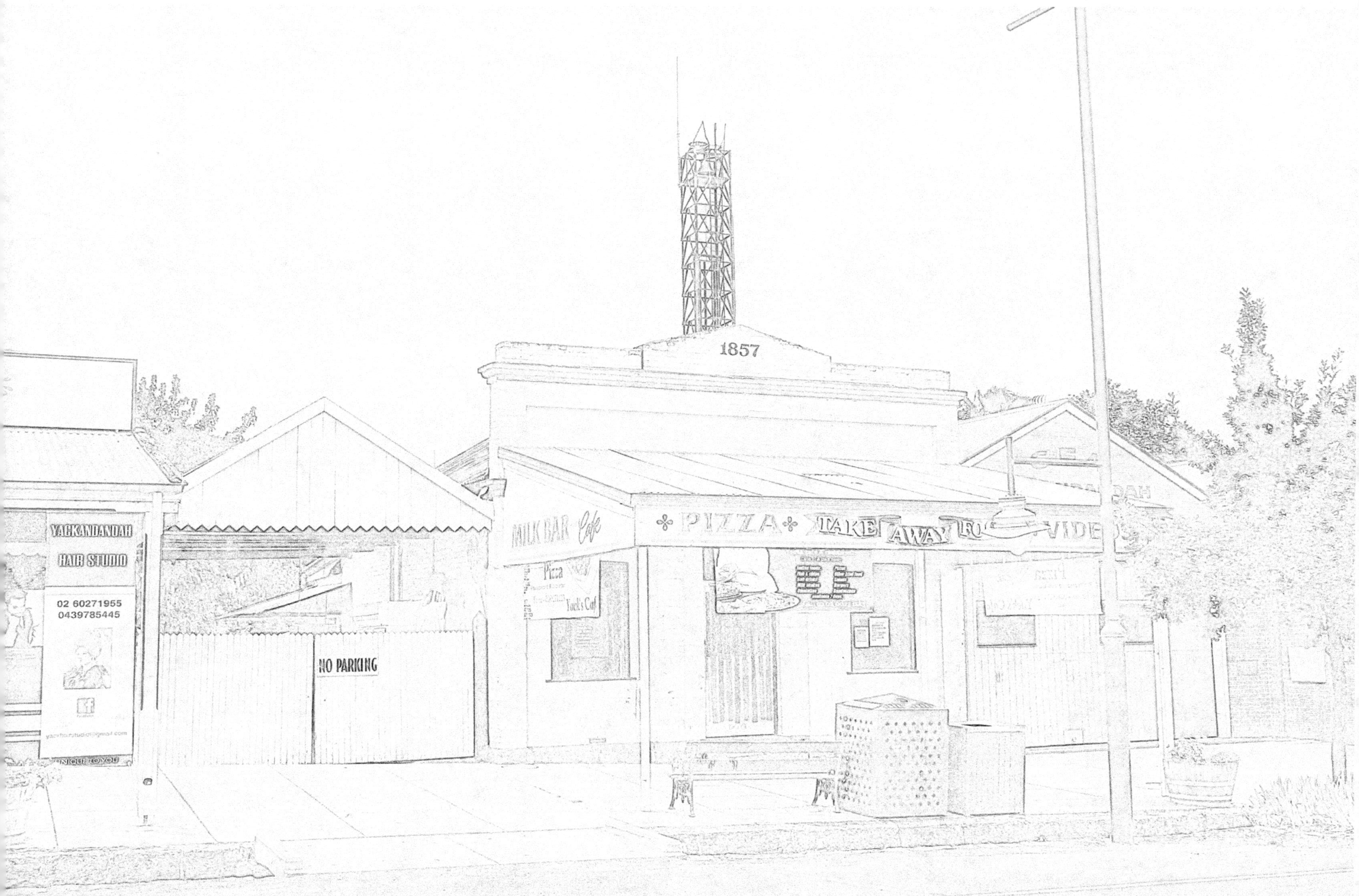
1857
MILK BAR Cafe
PIZZA
TAKE AWAY
YACKANDANDAH
HAIR STUDIO
02 60271955
0439785445
NO PARKING

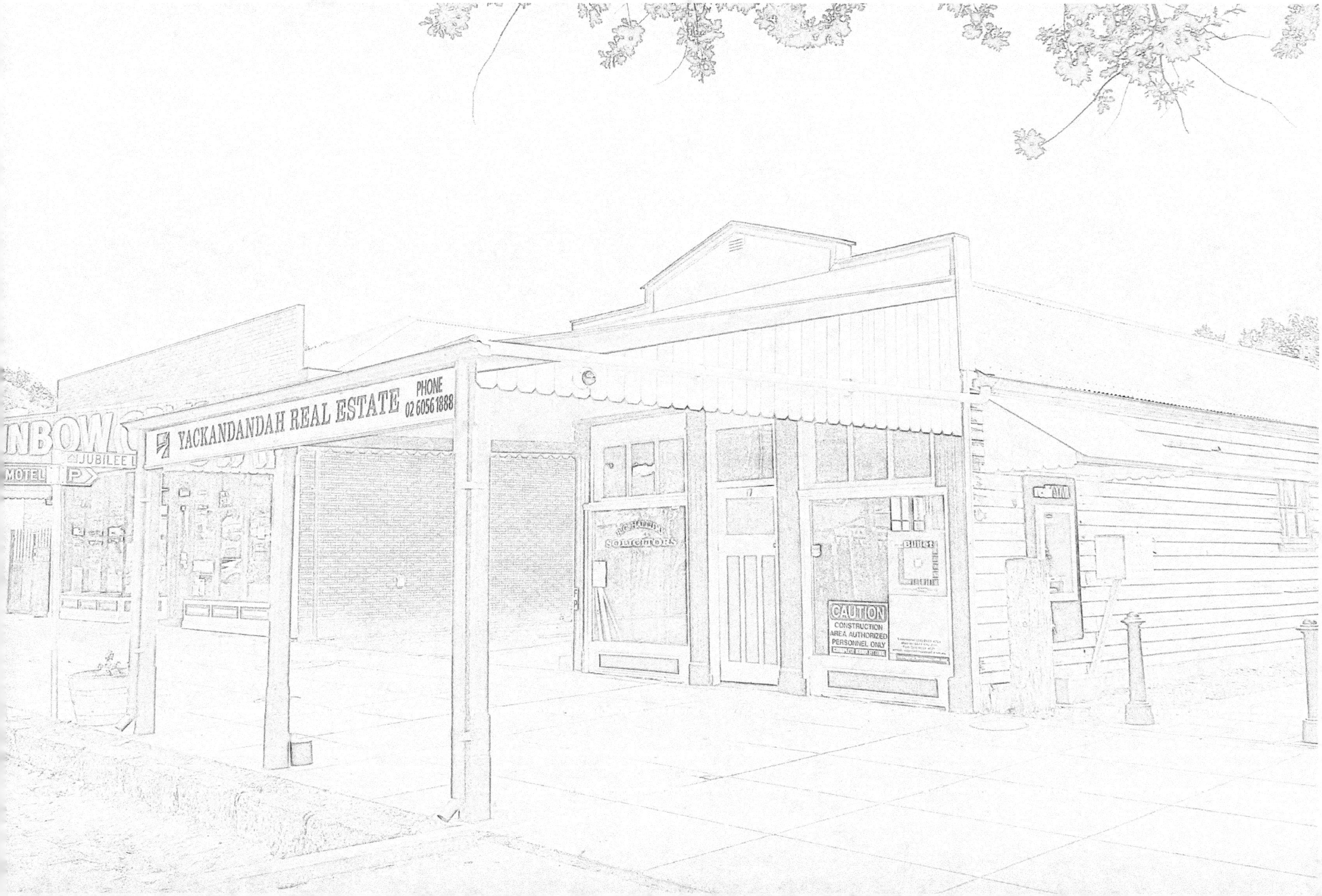

NBOW
JUBILEE
MOTEL
P
YACKANDANDAH REAL ESTATE
PHONE
02 6056 1888
SOLICITORS
CAUTION
CONSTRUCTION
AREA AUTHORIZED
PERSONNEL ONLY
Billet
ATM

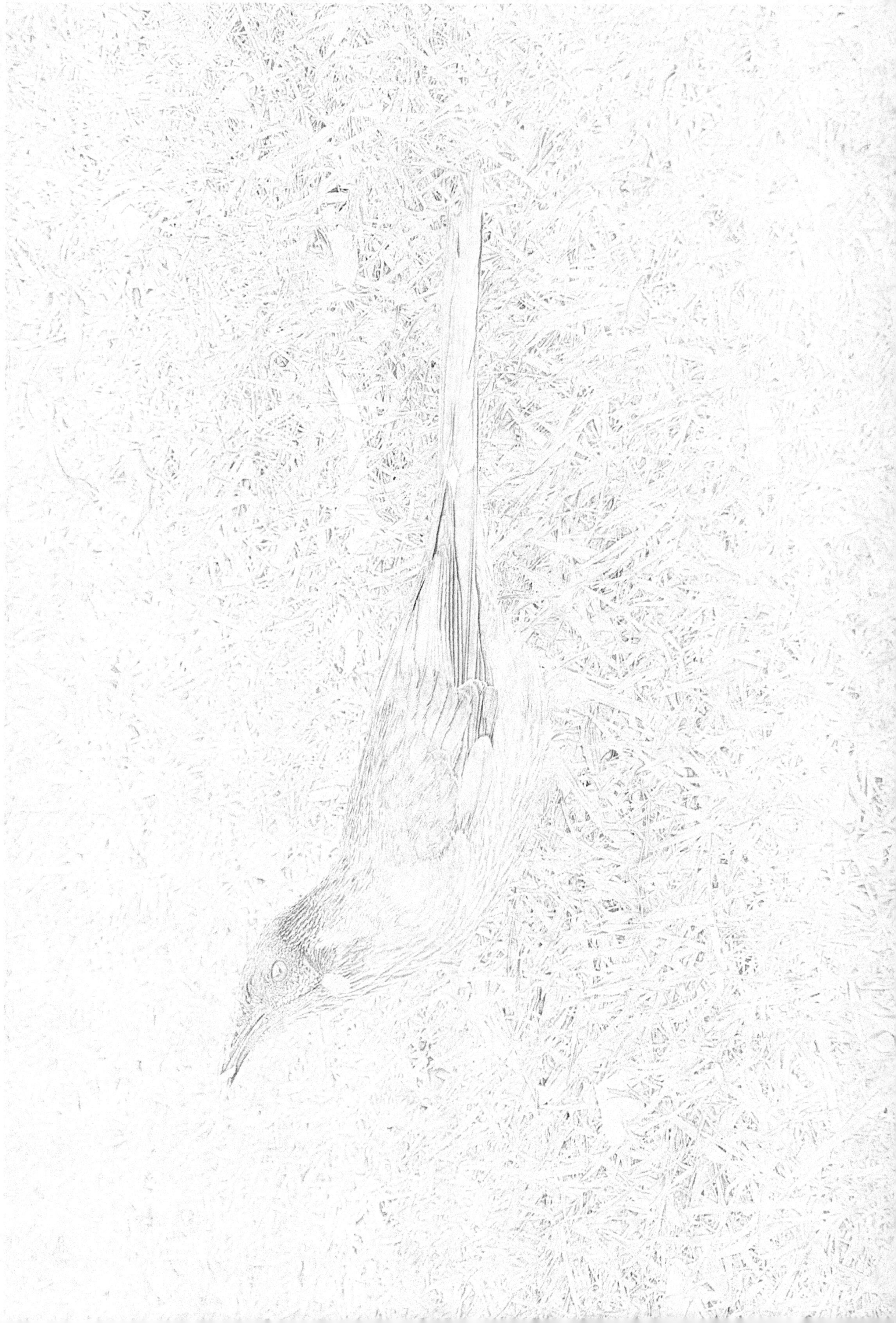

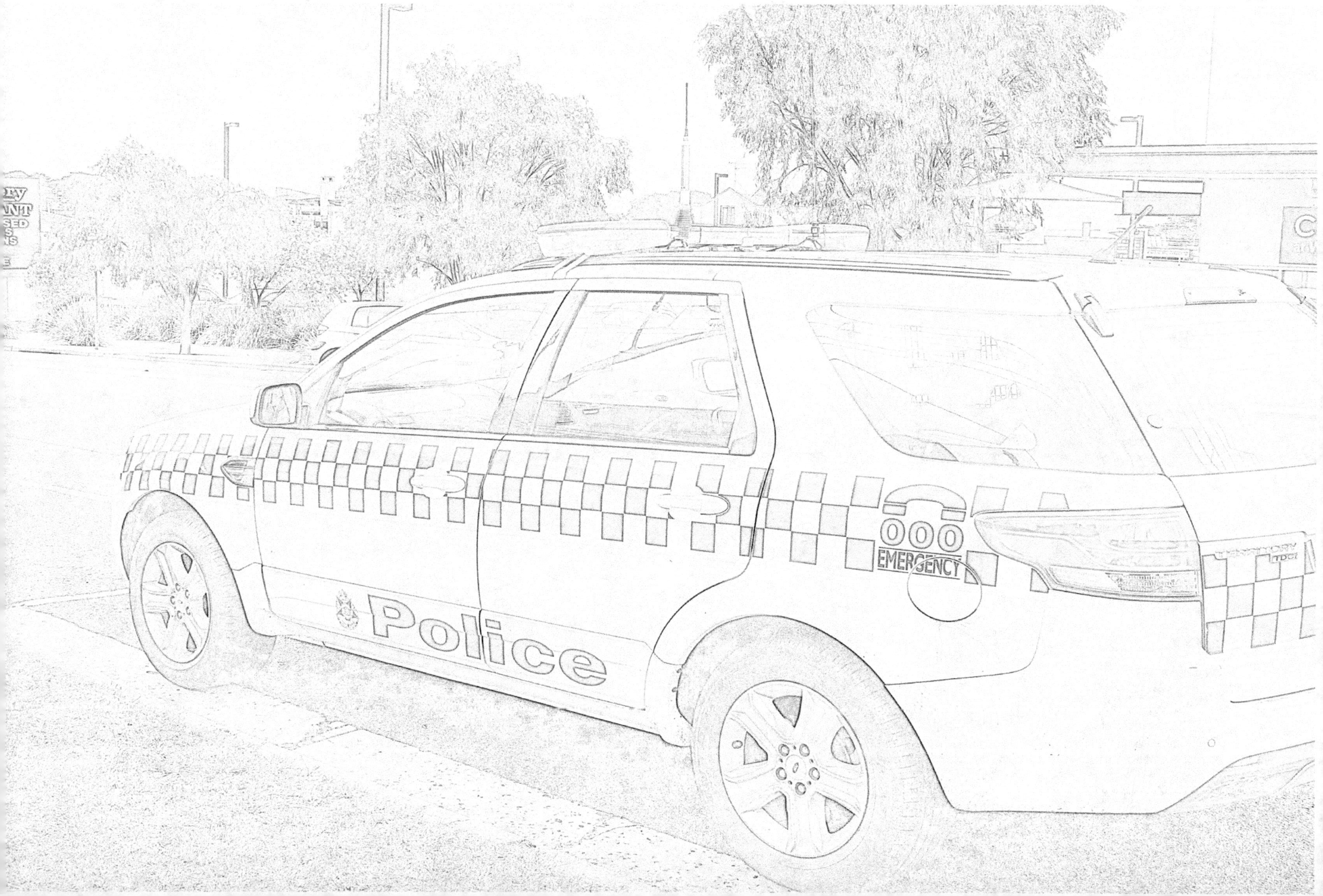
000
EMERGENCY
Police

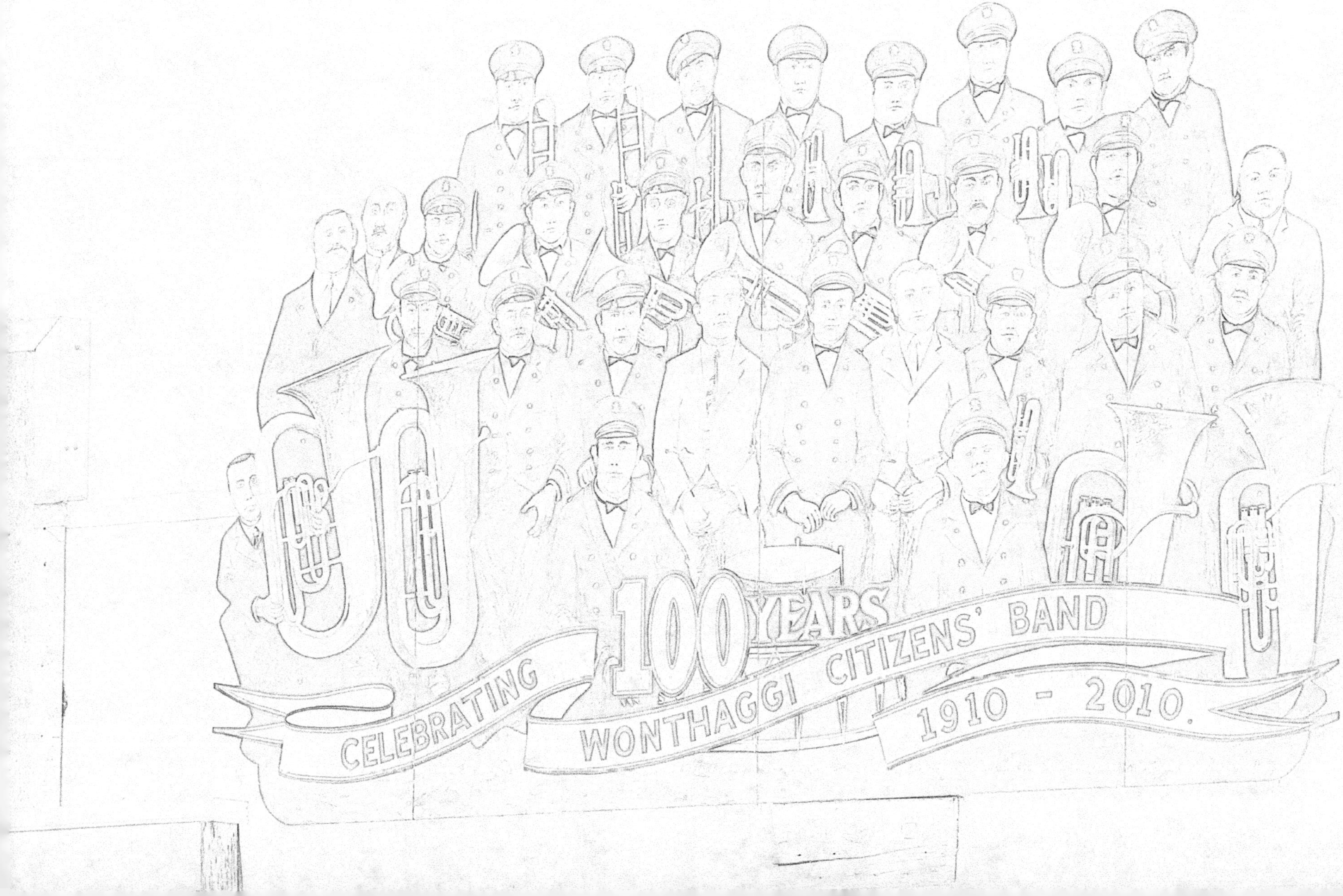
CELEBRATING
100 YEARS
WONTHAGGI CITIZENS' BAND
1910 - 2010.

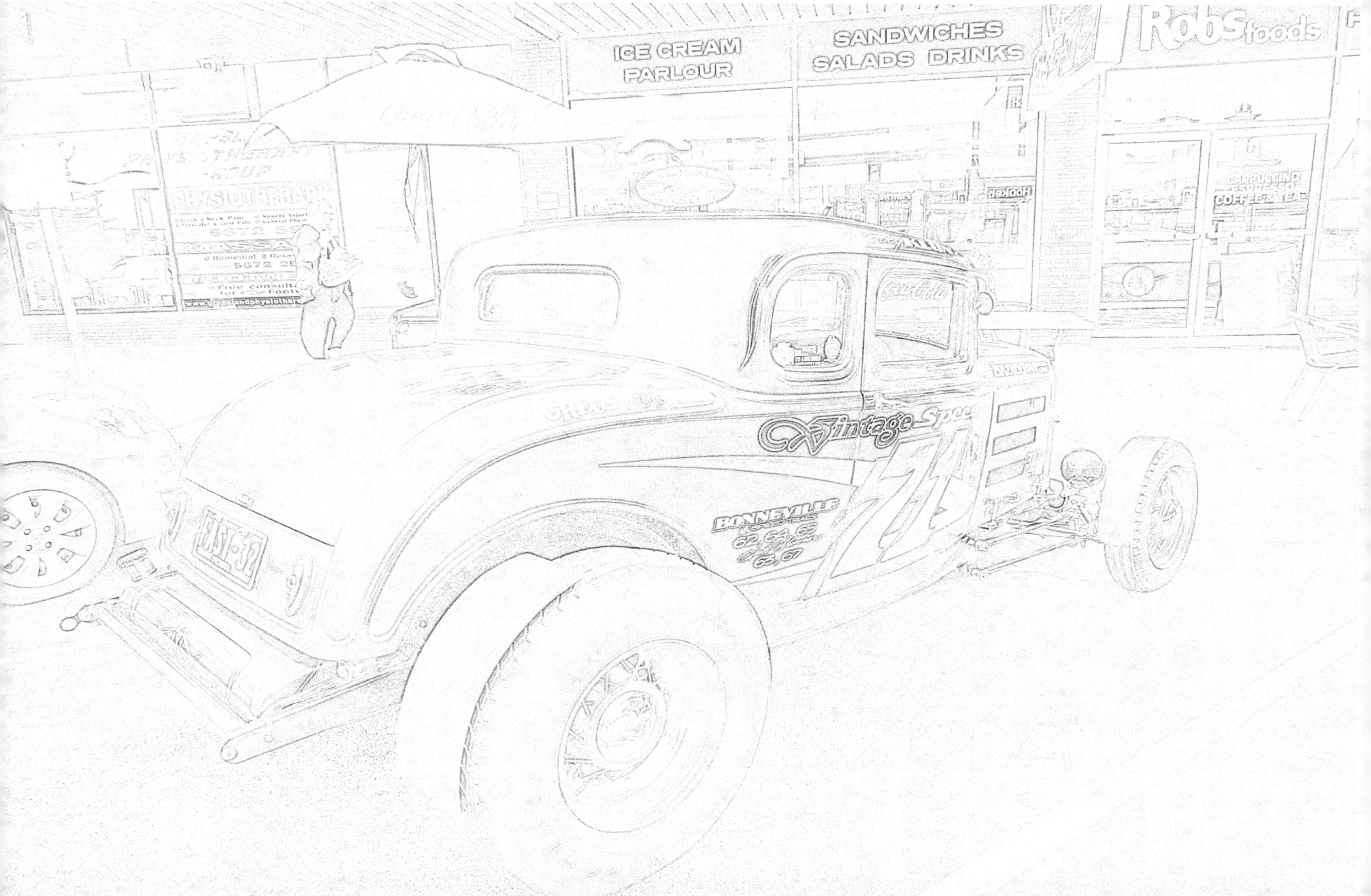
ICE CREAM
PARLOUR
SANDWICHES
SALADS DRINKS
Robs foods
CAPPUCCINO
ESPRESSO
COFFEE & TEA
PHYSIOTHERAPY
5672
FAST-32
BONNEVILLE
Vintage Speed
Coca-Cola

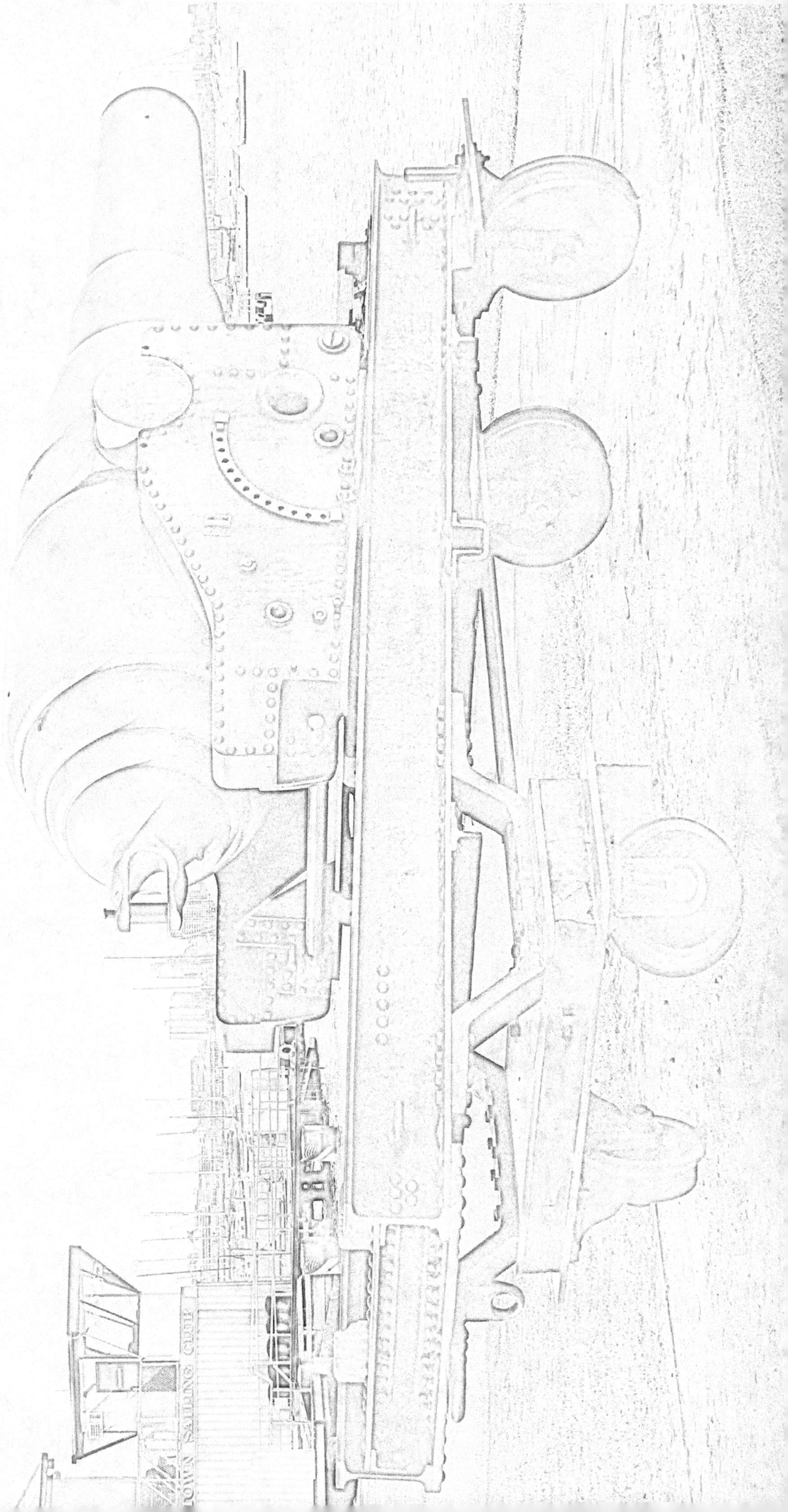
SAILING CLUB

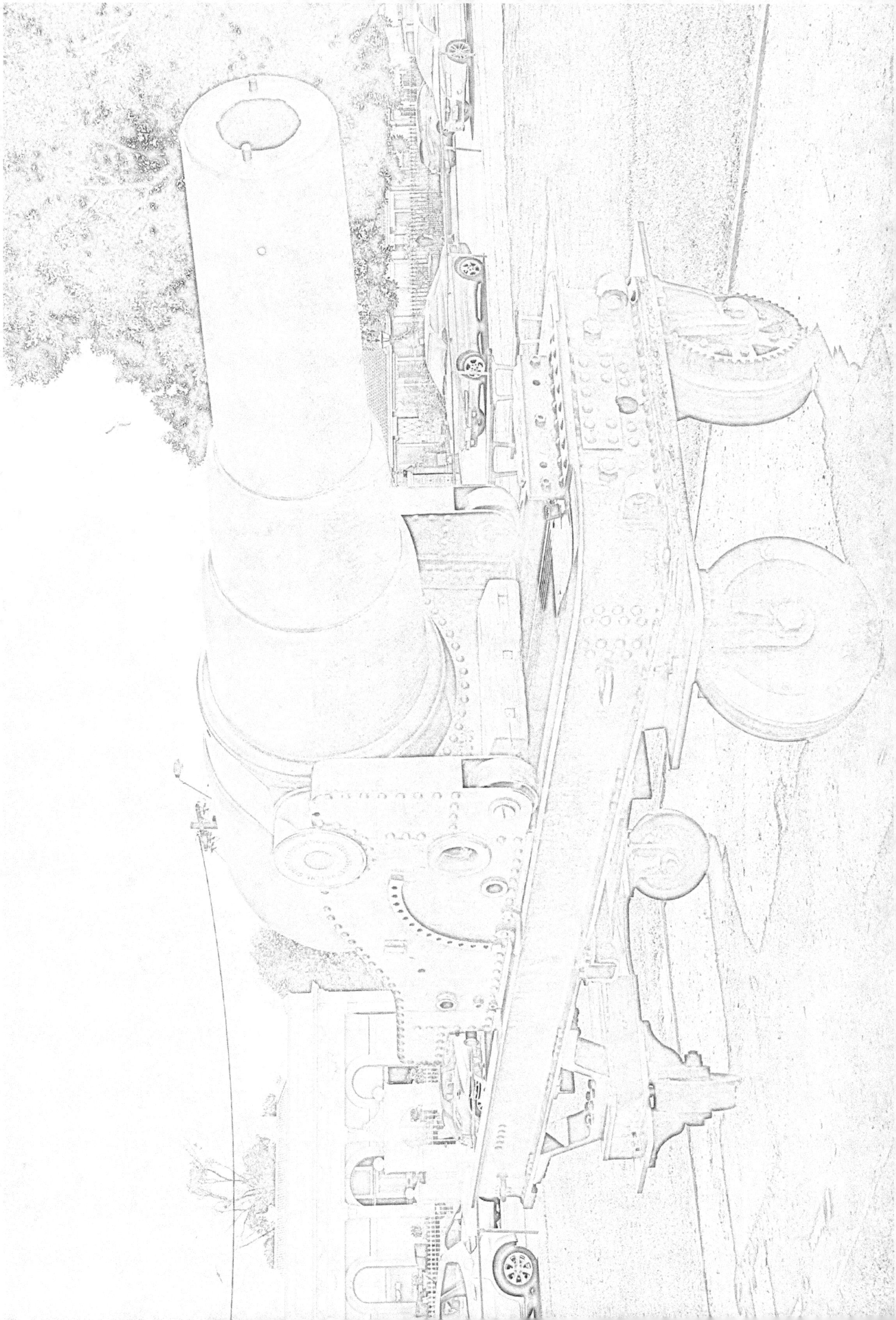

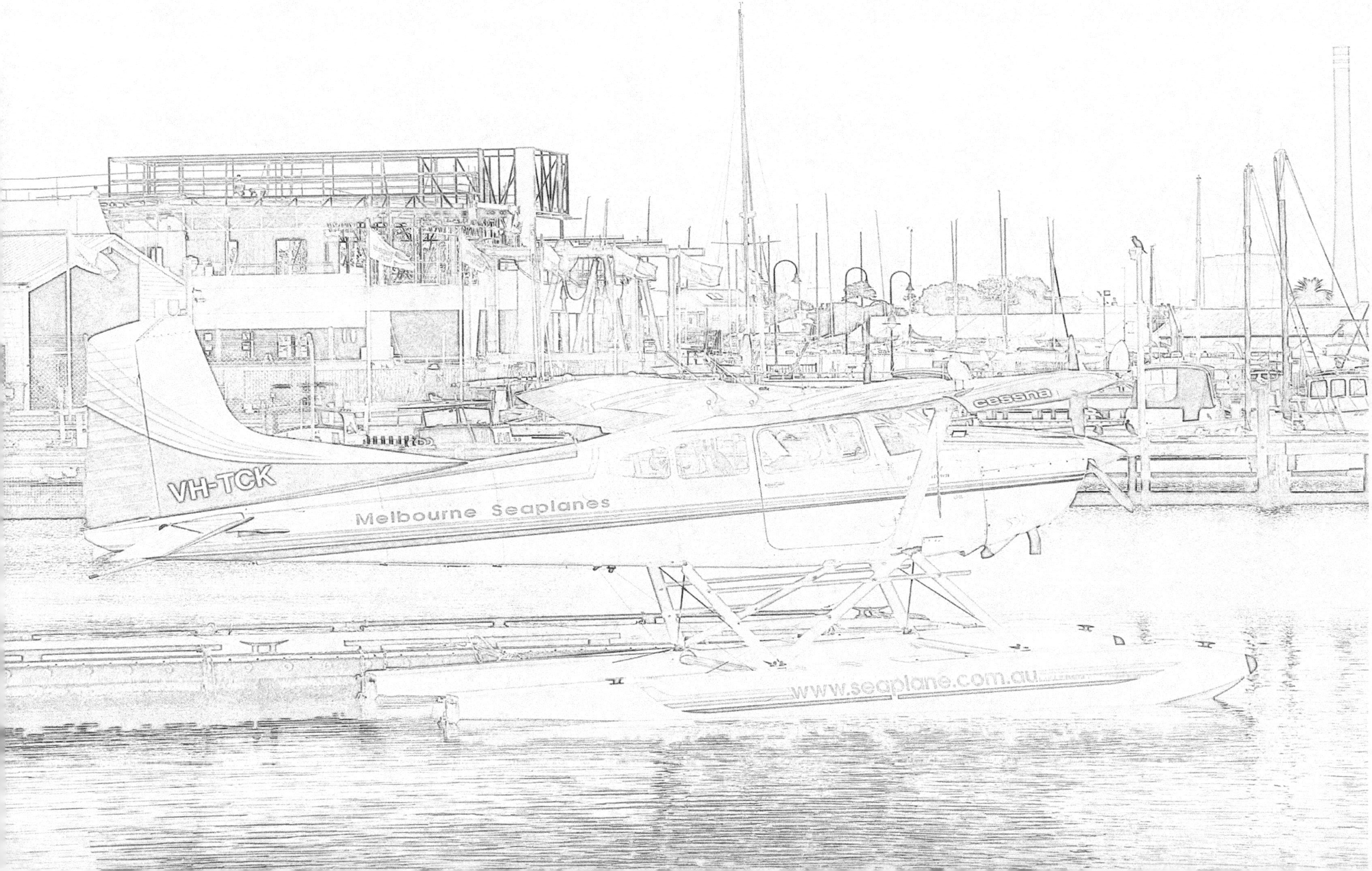
VH-TCK
Melbourne Seaplanes
cessna
www.seaplane.com.au

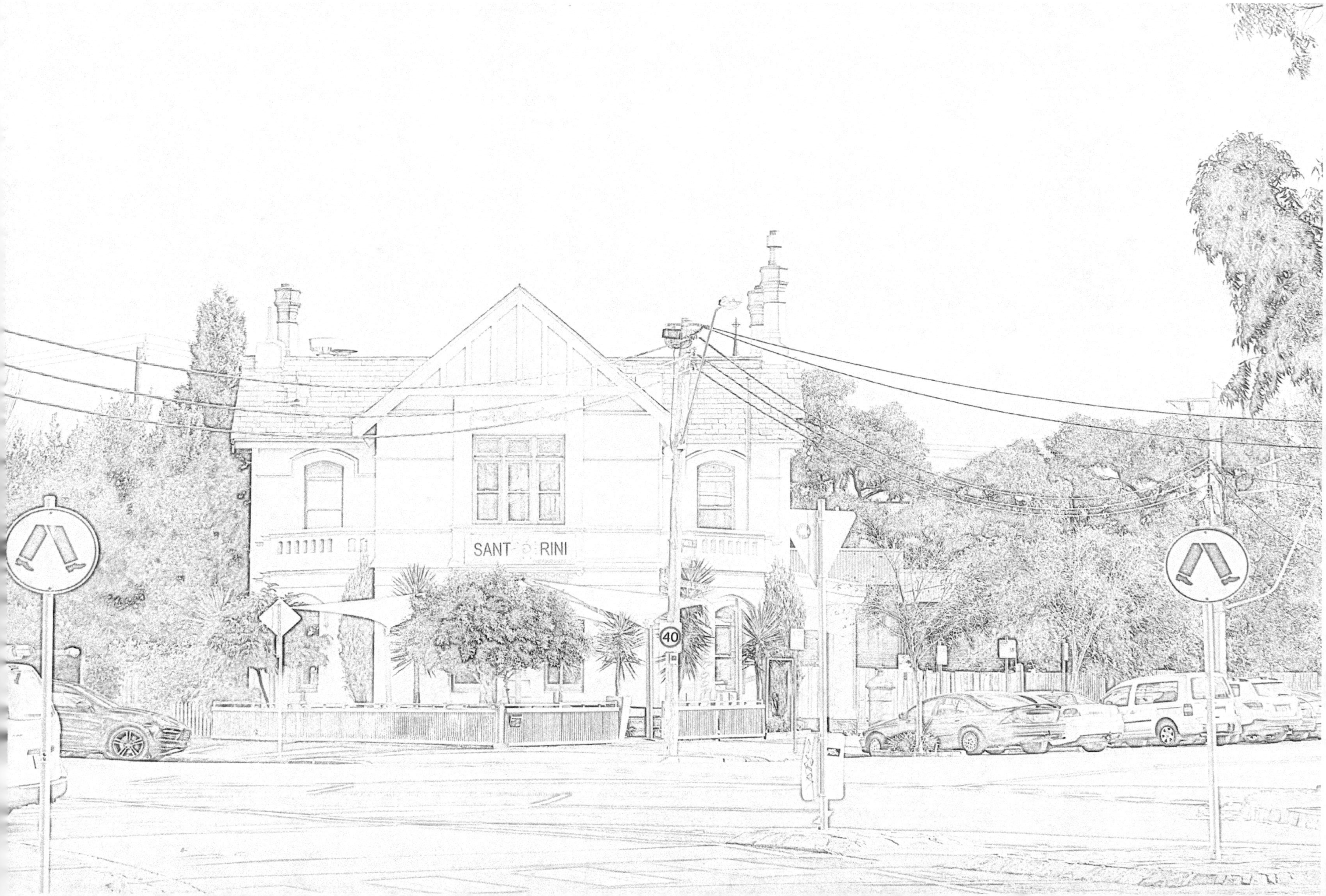

RINI
40

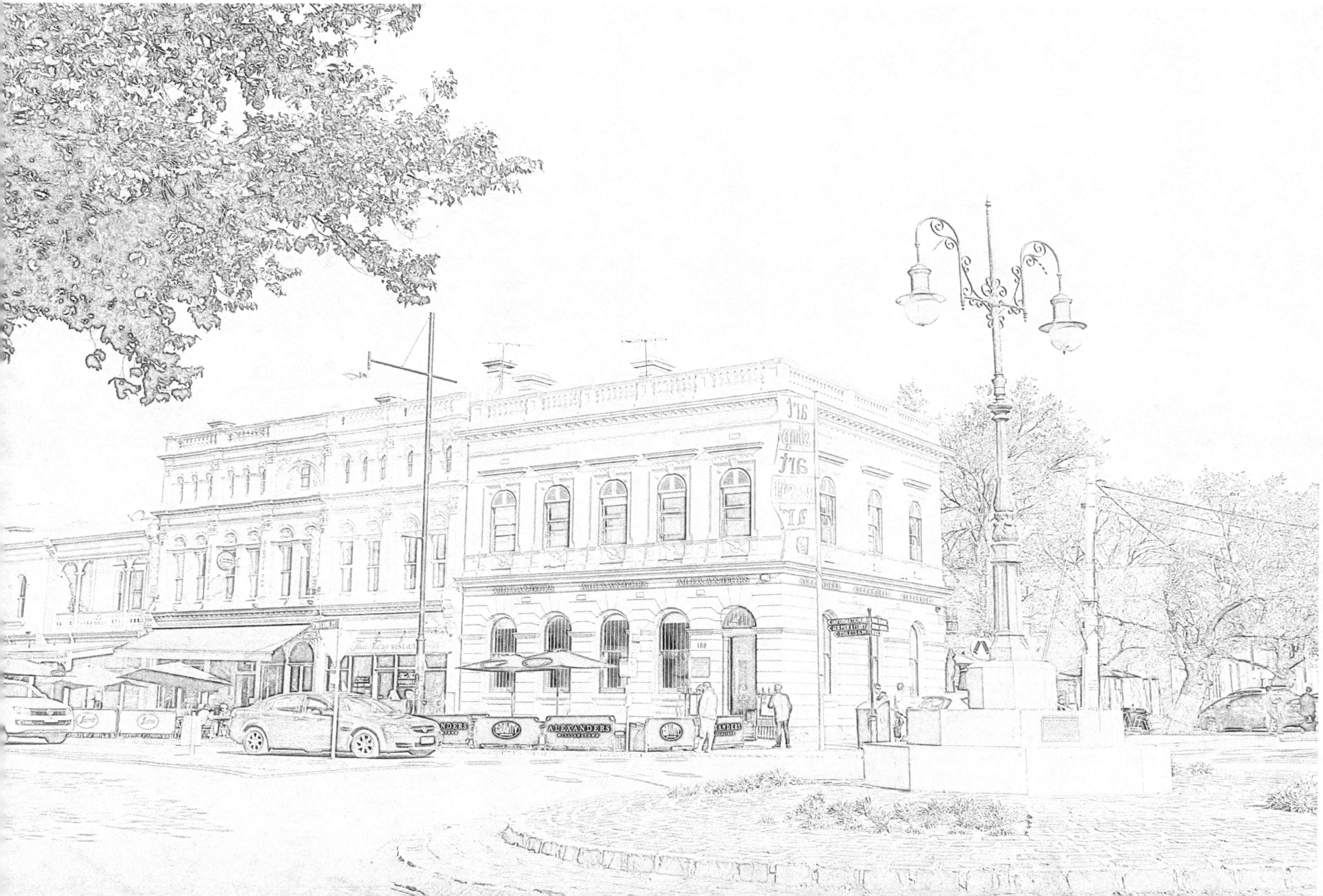
ALEXANDERS
ALEXANDERS
ALEXANDERS
189

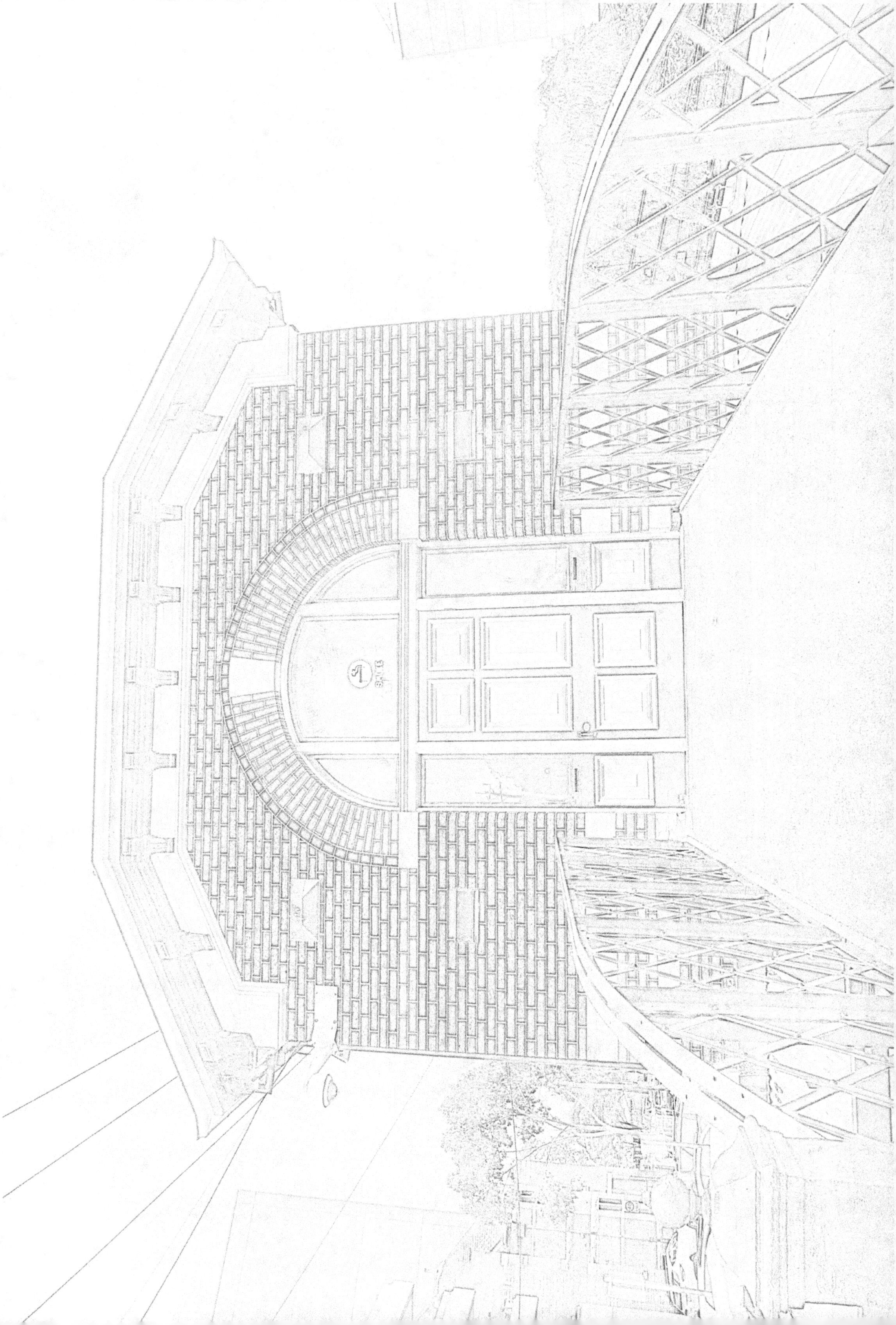

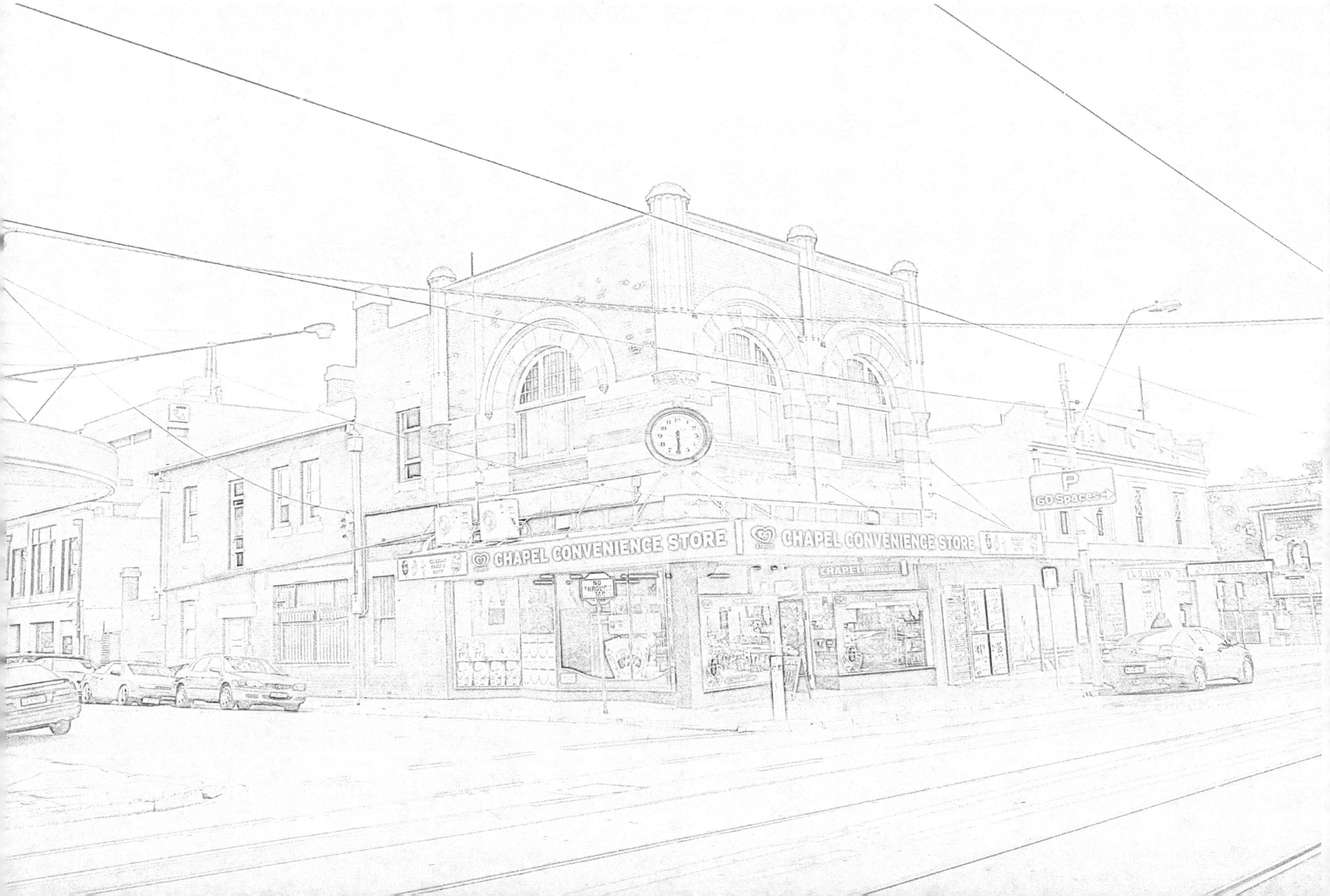
CHAPEL CONVENIENCE STORE
CHAPEL CONVENIENCE STORE
CHAPEL CONVENIENCE STORE
P
60 Spaces
NO THROUGH ROAD
CHAPEL

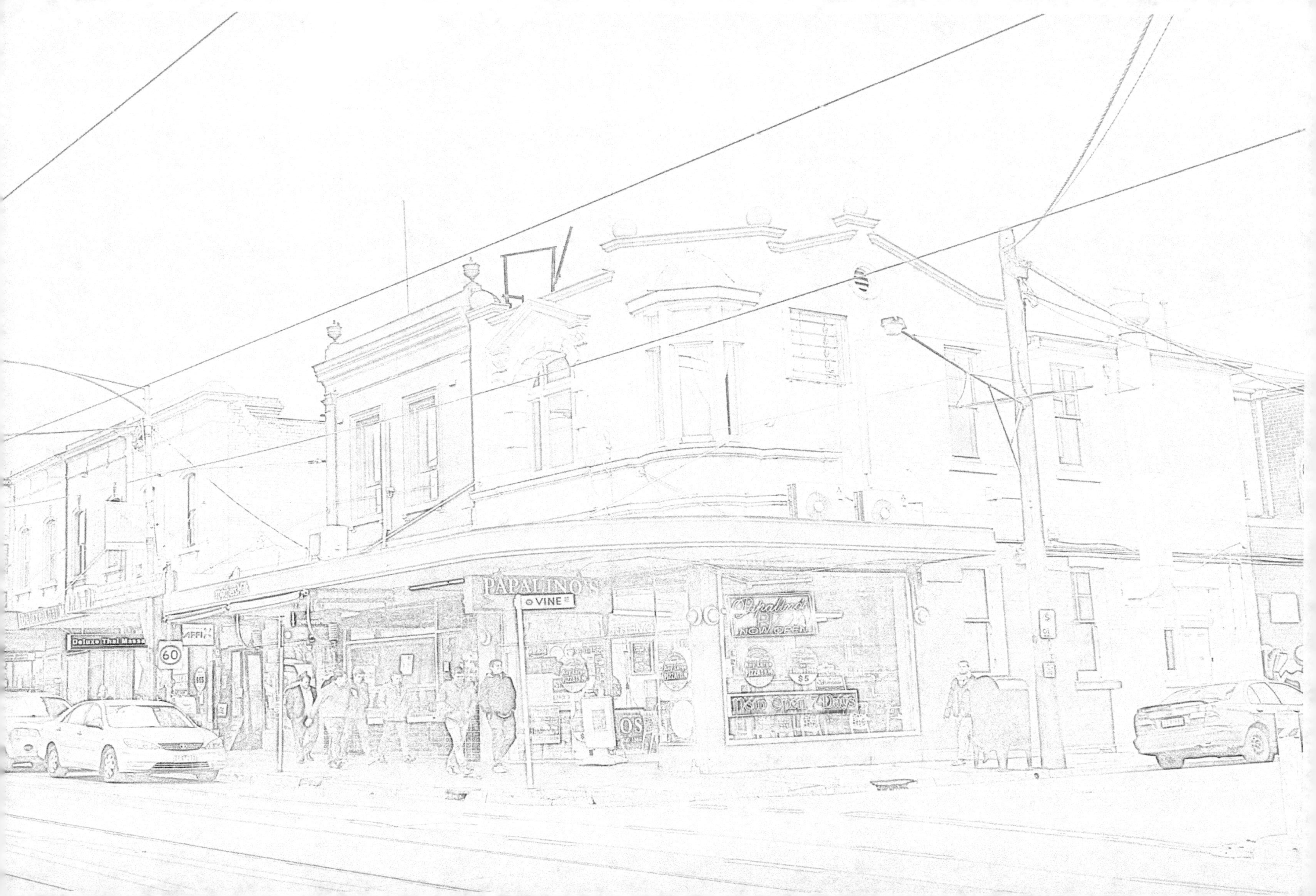
PAPALINO'S
VINE ST
NOW OPEN
$5
Now Open 7 Days
60
Deluxe Thai Massa

www.ingramcontent.com/pod-product-compliance
Lightning Source LLC
Chambersburg PA
CBHW081056180526
45170CB00005B/1777